Kuwait:
Fall and Rebirth

Kuwait:
Fall and Rebirth

Mohammed A. Al-Yahya

Kegan Paul International
London and New York

First published in 1993 by
Kegan Paul International Ltd
PO Box 256, London WC1B 3SW, England

Distributed by
John Wiley & Sons Ltd
Southern Cross Trading Estate
1 Oldlands Way, Bognor Regis
West Sussex, PO22 9SA, England

Routledge, Chapman & Hall Inc
29 West 35th Street
New York, NY 10001–2291, U.S.A.

Phototypeset in Palatino 10/12pt
by Intype, London
Printed in Great Britain by TJ Press, Padstow, Cornwall

ISBN 0 7103 0463 3

British Library Cataloguing in Publication Data
Al-Yahya, Mohammed
  Kuwait: Fall and Rebirth
  I. Title
  330.95367

ISBN 0–7103–0463–3

US Library of Congress Cataloging in Publication Data
Al-Yahya, Mohammed Abdulrahman, 1947–
  Kuwait: fall and rebirth/Mohammed Abdulrahman Al-Yahya
  130 pp. 220 cm.
  Includes index.
  ISBN 0–7103–0463–3
  1. Gulf Stock Exchange (Kuwait, Kuwait)—History. 2. Stock
exchange—Kuwait—History. 3. Sūq al-Munākh (Kuwait)—
History. 4. Iraq–Kuwait Crisis, 1990–1991—Economic aspects.
5. Kuwait—Economic conditions. I. Title.
HG5719.A3A4 1993
332.64'25367—dc20   93–15346
                                                          CIP

Dedicated to our martyrs who died
during the occupation of our country
and in the war of liberation, and to
our prisoners of war still remaining
in captivity

CONTENTS

PREFACE

The recent history of the Kuwait economy has been inextricably bound up with the history of oil. Oil has been the main source of the nation's wealth, but the health and vitality of the national economy depends firstly on how that wealth is utilised, and secondly on the way in which the national and private institutions combine to ensure the efficient regulation of national economic affairs. Kuwait's legal and governmental systems are based on principles which guarantee the freedom of the individual to pursue his or her economic advancement with the minimum state interference, and the national wealth is distributed in such a way as to facilitate this pursuit. Occasional aberrations are part of the price necessary to maintain this freedom, and the test of a nation's maturity lies not in whether such aberrations occur, but how its regulatory authorities are able to control them and limit their effects.

During the past decade Kuwait's economic development has been affected by two severe shocks – a collapse in an unofficial stock market in 1982, and the invasion in 1990 coupled with the subsequent war of liberation in the following year. These shocks occurred during a period in which other adverse economic and political events were impinging on the region: the falling price of oil and the Iran–Iraq war being the most prominent. How these shocks affected Kuwait, and especially its economic future, and how they were managed in order to limit their effects, form the common theme throughout this book which is written from the point of view of a banker with long experience in national economic affairs and who remained in Kuwait throughout the occupation.

Mohammed Abdulrahman Al-Yahya

ix

DOLLAR–DINAR EXCHANGE RATE

During the years 1982–1992, the annual average exchange rate of the Kuwaiti dinar in US dollars was as follows:

1982 (1 dinar =) 3.473 dollars
1983   3.431
1984   3.379
1985   3.324
1986   3.442
1987   3.586
1988   3.585
1989   3.404
1990   3.434
1991   3.458
1992   3.417

1

KUWAIT: A HISTORICAL PERSPECTIVE

Although there are some traces, and also a few hazy records, of earlier settlements in the region where modern Kuwait City now stands, the Kuwait we know had its beginnings during the later years of the eighteenth century, when a group of families moved out of the Najd, a region in the centre of the Arabian Peninsula, and settled in the area. Not that it could have been as completely desolate a spot as is often supposed. There were important trade routes crossing at or near what must have been the site of the first settlement, with camel trains from the north and east to Arabia and Africa intersecting at the head of the Gulf, and with much trade between Europe and the Indies and China crossing the Levant to and from the seaports on the Gulf's shore. It is thought, too, that trade between the area and the East Coast of Africa and other areas of the Indian Ocean was established quite early in Kuwait's modern history, but although more and more evidence of this and other matters is continually coming to light, little can be asserted with documentary precision. What is known, however, is that the original families which comprised the first settlement formed a closely knit community, and although they were joined by others during the following decades, that same close-knit community spirit has been a feature of Kuwait's development right up to the present day, with those same original families still forming the nucleus of much of the commercial, social and political life of the country.

During the years prior to the twentieth century it is evident that Kuwait's prosperity depended upon the sea. Very little agricultural land was available in the hinterland, and water was in very short supply, and although the early families from

1

the Najd would have had a pastoral background, Kuwaitis soon became famous as seafarers, with their distinctive trading dhows (known as booms) being common in the ports right down the East African coast and on the coasts of India and beyond to the shores of the Malay Peninsula. The boom was probably the ultimate development of the dhow, being fast and versatile, yet able to withstand the rigorous journeys which such trade necessitated. A commercial network developed on the basis of this trade, and many of the great commercial families of Kuwait set up trading establishments in the numerous ports of call around the coasts of the Indian Ocean, and also invested in date plantations and other sources of trade goods, primarily in Iraq, to supply them with the materials on which their commercial activities depended.

In those days ocean-going ships depended entirely on the wind for motive power, and during certain times of the year long journeys were not possible. Kuwaiti seafarers soon found another activity to employ their ships during such periods, and this was nearer home: it was pearling. The pearls of the Gulf were famous, and in the middle of the nineteenth century up to 600 boats might be seen over the pearling grounds during the pearling season. Kuwaiti boats would have formed a prominent part of the fleet. Dealing in pearls became an important activity in Kuwait, as did dealing in gold, which was the life-blood of the trade in goods which their booms were carrying across the seas. Whether trading or pearling, however, the Kuwaiti mariners endured a hard life indeed. Pearl diving was dangerous in the extreme, and regularly took its toll of those who practised the occupation, either through fatal accidents or through a degeneration of health due to the adverse conditions under which they worked. At the same time, trading voyages on the open sea necessitated long weeks and months in sailing craft which offered little protection from the elements and in which the supplies of food and water were both basic and limited. Small wonder, then, that the Kuwaiti people developed an independence and resilience unsurpassed in the region, and that by the end of the nineteenth century their prowess in trade and commerce had become renowned.

It was this trading past, as well as the history of their origin, which helped them shape a special form of social organisation which was to be so influential during later periods of economic development. The trading dynasties, based in the main on the founding families of the state, did not have the benefit of modern communications, so that a special form of trust had to be developed between members of the commercial community. Bargains would be struck without written contract, and credit and debts would often be of long duration. Commerce in Kuwait, therefore, was a very closely knit activity. Only those who proved their worth were tolerated, while those within the community could rely on fraternal support during times of individual adversity. The Diwania (that part of the larger Kuwaiti house set apart for the adult male members of the family to entertain male friends) became a centre for commercial as well as social discourse, just as the coffee houses of London had formed the basis of many of the great financial and commercial establishments of Britain in earlier times.

KUWAIT'S POLITICAL DEVELOPMENT

The early settlers in Kuwait elected their leader, or sheikh. Theirs was not a leadership established by the sword, and although necessarily powerful, Kuwait's early sheikhs held their power on behalf of the people. From those early times, the sheikhs were elected from the Sabah family, but a great deal of power inevitably resided with the large merchant families who provided the resources necessary for any government to be effective. The feudal system, in which the monarch allocated land to his vassals and thereby held effective control over the people and secured their service, was never present in Kuwait, and the frequent references to Kuwait as a 'feudal state' are fundamentally in error.[1] The system of government served the country well during the early period, in which as much commercial freedom as possible was required to allow commerce to flourish, yet providing a stable home base from which the commercial organisations could conduct their foreign activities.

It was toward the end of the nineteenth century, however, that Kuwait became important on the world political stage. That century had seen a tremendous surge in imperial developments by the industrialising countries of Europe, who required both raw materials and markets for their newly created and fast-growing industries. The Industrial Revolution had spawned new means of mechanical transport. Ships could cross the oceans independent of the vagaries of wind or weather, and railways could open up the hinterland of countries where hitherto trade had been conducted via coastal trading posts only. The vast resources discovered in many colonies needed transport to the home country, as did food supplies grown in the colonies to feed the factory workers in the newly created and rapidly growing industrial towns. The Suez Canal had been opened in the third quarter of the century, and the British, by their control of the canal, as well as their presence in Gibraltar, Malta, Cyprus and Aden, were in command of the sea routes through the Mediterranean and the Red Sea to East Africa and the Far East.

Britain had effectively controlled world commerce throughout the nineteenth century after the defeat of France at Waterloo in 1815, and the rise of other industrial countries in Europe from the middle of the century onward saw them trying to break the British strangle-hold on the world's major trade routes. Germany had formed alliances with a number of mid-European states, and also with Turkey, whose Ottoman Empire straddled the Levant. Through these alliances, Germany planned to build a railway through Eastern Europe, across Turkey and the Levant to the Gulf, thus breaking Britain's domination of the routes to the East.[2] Kuwait was the first, and best, choice for the terminal for this line, and Germany relied on Turkish hegemony in the area to bring this plan to fruition.

Meanwhile, during the final years of the century, Kuwait had been undergoing significant political change. In 1886 Sheikh Sabah II had died, to be succeeded by his son Abdullah, who only reigned for six years, to be followed by Mohammad, who ruled in conjunction with his brother Jarah. In 1896 their half-brother Mubarak seized control of the country, and by judicious diplomatic activity he succeeded in cementing friendships with the powerful families in the interior of the Arabian Peninsula. He also courted British interest, and in 1899 concluded a treaty with Britain accepting its protection. Under this treaty, Britain agreed to protect Kuwait's physical integrity in return for Kuwait's agreement not to lease, cede, or give concessions of any land to a foreign power without British acquiescence.[3] The relationship with Britain was maintained until 1961 when the Protection Agreement was terminated. Consequently, when, at the end of the First World War, the separate countries of the Middle East were given international recognition as independent states, the independence of Kuwait had already been officially recognised for over two decades. Although Mubarak died in 1915 he had already established the constitutional procedure by which the ruling sheikh, although still to be subject to national approval, was to be chosen from the Sabah family. He had thus firmly established the independence of his small but important sheikhdom, so that any claim by a modern state that Kuwait had once formed part of it, cannot be anything but spurious.

KUWAIT AND THE WORLD OIL MARKET

If Kuwait achieved importance at the end of the nineteenth century due to its strategic position at the top of the Gulf, its importance during the twentieth century has stemmed from a totally different source: oil. The history of oil and the history of modern Kuwait are inseparable.

Immediately prior to the First World War, the British Navy had decided, under the leadership of Winston Churchill as First Lord of the Admiralty, to change from coal to oil as its motive power. In 1913 Sheikh Mubarak permitted British representatives to survey areas of Kuwait for oil. The fascinating details of the following years can be read in *The First Kuwait Oil Concession* by A.H.T. Chisholm,[4] who was an active participant in the negotiations between the Anglo-Persian Oil Company and Sheikh Ahmad, who ruled from 1921 to 1950. A final agreement to permit the actual drilling for oil was not concluded until 1934, and it was not until four years later that oil was discovered.

The Second World War commenced in 1939, and although subsequent drilling showed exciting prospects, the wells were capped in 1942, and work was not recommenced until 1945 when the war was almost over. It was soon established that what is now known as the Burgan Oilfield in Kuwait was the largest known oilfield in the world, and that together with some smaller surrounding fields it contained 11 per cent of the known reserves of the non-communist world. Export of oil commenced in 1946, and Table 1.1 shows the magnitude of the rate of increase of oil output over the succeeding years to 1977, together with the size of the revenues which the export of this oil generated. (It should be noted that during the earlier part of the period the price of oil was low, and its sale revenue, after deducting the cost of production, was shared according to varying formulae between the exploiting companies and the government of Kuwait. Only after the completion of nationalisation in 1976 did the whole of the sale proceeds accrue to the country itself.)[5]

Table 1.1 Crude oil output and Government revenues 1946–77

Year	Output (million US barrels)	Revenues (million US dollars)
1946	5.9	0.76
1947	16.2	2.07
1948	46.5	5.95
1949	89.9	11.52
1950	125.7	16.09
1955	402.7	281.7
1960	619.1	445.8
1965	861.5	567.5
1970	1090.6	784.0
1971	1116.4	963.0
1972	1201.6	1650.0
1973	1102.5	1795.2
1974	929.3	7094.9
1975	760.7	8641.2
1976	785.2	9802.8
1977	718.0	8963.1

Source: M.W. Khouja and P.G. Sadler, The Economy of Kuwait, London, Macmillan, 1979.

Up to 1961, Kuwait's external relationships had been conducted according to the Protection Agreement with Great Britain, but it must be stressed that this agreement had been concluded between two sovereign states by mutual consent. It in no way implied that Kuwait was to enjoy a subordinate status as a result of it. In fact, it was the independence of Kuwait which Great Britain was agreeing to protect. Throughout the period of the agreement's existence, as Al Ibraheem notes,[6] 'The Political Agent has never been called upon to make representation to the ruler of Kuwait affecting the internal administration of the Principality. Gunboats and aeroplanes have protected [Kuwait] . . . but no troops have ever been landed. In no part of the Gulf have relationships of the Sheikh and his people with the British Government and its representatives been more widely pleasant and cordial.'

In 1961 Kuwait was admitted to the United Nations. By then, it was already a prominent member of OPEC, and had become one of the world's leading oil producers. Oil, and the financial status which oil revenues later provided, were to give Kuwait a prominence in world affairs which belied both its geographical size and its very small population.

POPULATION GROWTH AND SOCIAL DEVELOPMENT

Data on Kuwait's population prior to the Second World War is comparatively scarce. Visiting scholars sometimes made estimates based on observation rather than research, and it was never known how many of those observed were indigenous residents and how many were transitory workers or traders, nor how many indigenous residents were abroad on trading voyages or were over the pearling grounds. The first reliable estimate was made in 1946, when the population was put at around 90,000. The first full census was taken in 1957, and from 1965 onward a census had been taken every five years (see Table 1.2).

Table 1.2 The population of Kuwait (in 000s)

Census year	Kuwaitis			Non-Kuwaitis			Total		
	Male	Female	Total	Male	Female	Total	Male	Female	Total
1957	59	55	114	73	20	93	132	74	206
1960	85	78	163	116	43	159	201	121	322
1965	113	107	220	174	74	248	287	181	468
1970	176	172	348	244	147	391	420	319	739
1975	252	251	503	323	240	563	575	491	1066
1980	281	285	566	496	296	792	777	581	1358
1985	339	342	681	626	390	1016	965	732	1697
1989 (estimated)	397	400	797	762	490	1252	1159	890	2049

Source: Annual Statistical Abstracts, Central Statistical Office, Kuwait.

By any standard, the rate of population growth has been phenomenal. This has resulted from two main forces: (i) the early willingness of the Kuwaiti Government to give Kuwaiti nationality to many of the previously nomadic people still living in its non-urban areas, and (ii) later, to give nationality to non-nationals who had lived in Kuwait for some years and who had contributed to the state's advancement.

Ever since the commencement of oil production it was the intention of Kuwait to use its wealth for the ultimate benefit of its citizens, while at the same time recognising its responsibilities to the world community. As mentioned earlier, Kuwait was never a feudal monarchy, where the country's wealth is at the disposal of the monarch. Kuwait's oil revenues accrue to the state itself, and their subsequent use, as with all other state revenues, is decided by the Council of Ministers. The Amir (as the sheikh is now known) is the guardian of the constitution. He has the power to suspend the constitution, and has done so in periods of national emergency, but there is no doubt that right up to the time of the Iraqi invasion Kuwait had been progressing towards a form of democracy compatible with western ideals while remaining true to its Islamic traditions and keeping faith with its historical genesis.

Ever since the flow of oil wealth commenced, education, housing and health have been given urgent priority. All Kuwaiti nationals have free access to education at all levels. The provision of education within the state runs from nursery to university status, and education abroad at university and other specialist levels is available for all those who are qualified to benefit from it. Hospital and clinical facilities are among the most modern in the world, and in practice are available to all within Kuwait's borders, irrespective of nationality, while treatment abroad is available to all nationals who require it. Housing construction has been encouraged by cheap loans to low-income families to enable them to purchase houses built at heavily subsidised prices. In addition, basic foodstuffs have been subsidised, and cheap power and water made available. A state social security system ensures pensions for older citizens and those otherwise incapacitated. All these provisions have been funded from the state's oil revenues, and have been one of the means by which these revenues have been distributed among the people.

One of the great problems inherent in any such system of state welfare, provided as it is without recourse to taxation, is the tendency for an attitude of dependency to develop among the population. This has been constantly in the minds of many, especially throughout the 1970s, when the burgeoning of oil revenues made more and more state funds available. But under a law adopted in August 1976, a Reserve Fund for Future Generations was established with an initial capital of KD 850 million. To this must be added 10 per cent of all state revenues during each year, and all interest accruing to it has to remain within the fund.

Also, in 1961, one of the first acts of the Kuwaiti Government after the cessation of the protectorate agreement was to set up the Kuwait Fund for Arab Economic Development. A proportion of all state revenues is allocated to this fund also, and after the oil price adjustments of 1973 the fund's scope was widened to include all developing countries. The Kuwait Fund has since grown to be one of the world's foremost aid-giving agencies, distributing hundreds of millions of dollars each year, and has been the model on which other national funds have been developed throughout the world.

Kuwait has always been both outward- and forward-looking, therefore, and has been mindful of its responsibilities to the world at large and to its own future citizens yet unborn. This volume deals with some of the traumatic experiences of the country over the last decade, some caused by internal forces arising from the allocation and use of its wealth, others by outside forces arising from the avarice of some who would wish to gain control of that wealth to serve their own ulterior ends.

DEVELOPMENT OF KUWAIT'S FINANCIAL SYSTEM

It seems incredible that it was not until 1961 that Kuwait commenced the distribution of its own currency, the Kuwaiti dinar. Up to that time the currency used was the Indian rupee, but in the immediate years prior to the introduction of the dinar trade in the rupee had been restricted to a special issue for use in the Gulf only (due largely to illegal trade in gold which had caused a drain on the ordinary rupee). The rupee was purchased by the Kuwaiti Government in exchange for sterling from the Reserve Bank of India, and surplus rupees could be changed back to sterling on demand.

The dinar was issued through the newly established Currency Board, and this continued in operation until the Central Bank of Kuwait was established in 1968. By this date, four commercial banks had been established, three insurance companies, and two investment companies. At that time the role of the financial system itself was limited, as the fiscal authorities would arrange through the Currency Board to exchange foreign currency for dinars in sufficient quantity to meet its domestic needs. It was not until these found their way into the hands of the public that they entered the financial system proper, and then they were mostly used to finance imports from abroad or foreign investment, or were sent abroad as remittances by foreign workers.

From 1970 onward the financial sector increased in size rapidly. Oil wealth was increasing due to increase in oil prices and the gradual nationalisation of oil resources and their exploitation, and the Government adopted a policy of investing abroad all revenues surplus to requirements, setting up specialist institutions to handle the sums available. It also enacted legislation forbidding foreign banks from operating on Kuwaiti soil, but at the same time adopted a policy of directing its foreign investments through local financial institutions. Later on in the decade, due to the increase in wealth of the general citizenry, more and more of the newly created institutions found themselves handling private funds for foreign investment, and also financing contractors engaged in the enormous growth in local infrastructure developments, so that many grew within a few years to be numbered among the largest of their kind in the Middle East.

FINANCIAL REGULATION

Due to the unique circumstances surrounding the formation of Kuwait's financial sector, and the speed with which it was accomplished, control of monetary operations had to be introduced gradually. There was no immediate model which could be followed, and measures were generally introduced as difficulties arose. It should be borne in mind that there was no national debt whereby Government paper could be held in the system and its discount rate altered according to financial policy. There was no income tax which could be manipulated to control inflationary demand, and the economy was completely open for the transfer in and out of foreign exchange. Net Government expenditure was the main determinant of the money supply, and the openness of the economy allowed surplus funds to be transferred out and to be spent or invested abroad with ease. The rapid growth in the non-oil economy occasioned by the large sums injected through Government spending on development within the country saw a rapid increase in the funds available to the private sector, and the financial base of the commercial banking system expanded accordingly. This expansion was most rapid after the oil price adjustments of 1973.

The ready availability of credit, a Government restriction on interest charges, and a rapidly expanding economy, all conspired to encourage borrowing, and it must be remembered that during much of the 1970s the world economy was also expanding rapidly. Oil receipts of the main oil producing countries were far exceeding their capacities to absorb them, and the transfer of funds abroad, both by private individuals and Governments in those countries, was keeping world interest rates low, encouraging rapid expansion, and fuelling inflation in the industrial world to such an extent that the purchasing power of Kuwait's oil receipts was rapidly being eroded. There was little opportunity, therefore, for any effective Government intervention at the domestic level to curb price increases, while rising incomes and the ready availability of credit combined to form a positive incentive to speculation.

THE KUWAIT STOCK MARKET

Up to 1977 there were only forty-two public shareholding companies in Kuwait, and the majority of these had been formed within the previous seven years. The total par value in 1977 was around KD 110 million. The then current market value, however, was KD 2.1 billion, such was the smallness of the number of shares available and the high level of demand. From 1970 to 1973 share prices increased threefold, and there was a further 125 per cent increase from that year to 1976. In 1977 this boom came to an end, and prices reduced rapidly, with many share values falling by 40 per cent. This led to Government intervention to support the market through an agreement to buy shares at a declared floor price in order to prevent

11

market values falling still further. A formal stock exchange was opened in the same year, as previously the market had relied on brokers' offices and relatively inadequate sources of information. On the Stock Exchange, as in banking and other major commercial activities, only Kuwaiti nationals were allowed to operate. The wealth of the nation was encouraged to circulate, but essentially within and among the indigenous population.

THE EARLIER YEARS IN RETROSPECT

This brief review of some salient points in Kuwait's history and progress serves to illustrate how the foundations of present-day Kuwait were established. Progress has been rapid. Within two generations Kuwait has been transformed from a small sheikhdom into an oil-rich state of world stature whose financial institutions operate in all of the world's major financial markets. Yet these recent developments have taken place against a historical background which has moulded a closely knit community with a unique system of inter-relationships built up through social as well as commercial intercourse. On the maintenance of these relationships has often depended the survival of the state. It is the way in which a country deals with adversity which is the real test of statehood, and without understanding the crucial role of these relationships in the past it is not possible to understand the attitudes which have dictated Kuwait's policies in the face of the adversities which the country has recently faced.

NOTES

1 For greater detail, see H.A. Al Ibraheem, *Kuwait, A Political Study*, Kuwait University, 1975.
2 See E.M. Earle, *Turkey, the Great Powers, and the Baghdad Railway*, New York, Macmillan, 1923.
3 See Al Ibraheem, *op. cit.*
4 See A.H.T. Chisholm, *The First Kuwait Oil Concession*, London, Frank Cass, 1975.
5 See Khouja and Sadler, *op. cit.*, pp. 177 *et seq.*
6 See Al Ibraheem, *op. cit.*

2

THE PRELUDE TO THE STOCK MARKET COLLAPSE

INTRODUCTION

During the last ten to twelve years this small country, Kuwait, tucked away at the top of the Arabian Gulf, has experienced a series of adverse financial, political and economic traumas out of all proportion to its limited size. Furthermore, the consequences of the turmoil created by these traumas have sometimes had repercussions throughout the world. It is inevitable that analysts and others of differing persuasions should vary in the emphasis they give to each element of the complicated web of forces which have impinged on the country during this period of its history, but this book is an attempt to elucidate and explain two of four major traumatic events of the last twelve years as seen through the eyes of a banker, to analyse their causes and patterns of development, and to offer suggestions for the solution of problems they have created wherever possible.

The four traumatic events which have given rise to the turmoil were:

1 A sustained drop in the world price of oil, and a marked reduction in the demand for oil throughout the 1980s. These factors signalled the end of the oil boom years, and their coming has seen a sustained decline in Kuwait's annual gross domestic product.

2 The prolonged war between Iran and Iraq, which lasted for eight of the twelve years.

3 A local stock market crisis, in which post-dated cheques worth more than US$ 90 billion were found to be circulating in the stock exchange system. Their total value exceeded the

13

total external debts of some of the then highest debtor
nations in the Third World, such as Mexico and Brazil.

4 And most significantly of all, the invasion and occupation of
Kuwait by Iraq and the ensuing war. The occupation lasted
only seven months, but no other country in the world has
experienced such a systematic attempt by one nation to eliminate the social structure, culture and economy of another. By
invading Kuwait on 2 August 1990 the Iraqi leader, Saddam
Hussein, sought more than just Kuwait's oil wealth. He
sought to eradicate its very identity as a nation. Blinded by
his greed and fed by his own illusions, Saddam confidently
believed that the nations of the world, after an initial period
of ritual protest, would come to terms with his blackmail and
that his loud rhetoric, so effective in securing the adulation of
his own ecstatic supporters at home, would be equally effective on the peoples of other countries. Thus, he hoped that
his bogus claims on Kuwait's territory would eventually
receive international acceptance. But this did not happen.
Kuwait did not find itself alone in its fight for survival.
Virtually the whole world rallied under the banner of the
United Nations to build a strong consensus against the Iraqi
dictator, who ultimately lost miserably to the US-led international forces. Saddam, who threatened to wage 'The
Mother of All Battles', quickly suffered 'The Mother of All
Defeats'.

While all the four issues listed had significant effects upon
Kuwait and its future development, the Iran–Iraq war, in both
its instigation and eventual termination, was essentially a political event, with very serious economic consequences. This was
true also of the collapse of oil prices, in that the recession
which caused it and the international attempts to diversify fuel
use away from oil were both politically instigated as major oil
users sought to control inflation and worsening balance of
payments deficits. Both traumas were world events which had
serious implications for Kuwait. However, in the case of the
Stock Market crisis (or Al Manakh, as it came to be known) the
issue was of essentially local importance, with some spillover
of effects into neighbouring Gulf Co-operation Council states,
notably Saudi Arabia and Bahrain. The Gulf War and its after-
math, of course, was the most significant event of the four,

both from its local importance to Kuwait and also its importance in a world-wide context.

This book is primarily addressed to the last two mentioned,
the Stock Market crisis and the Gulf War, and concludes with
an analysis of some post-liberation scenarios, which by the
nature of the problems created by each have to take both major
events into acocunt.

AL MANAKH – THE STOCK MARKET CRISIS

The word 'Manakh' has an interesting origin. 'Aukh' was the
word of command the old Beduin people addressed to their
camels to instruct them to lower themselves to the ground
when laden. In pre-oil times the Beduin from the surrounding
desert would come into the City of Kuwait and congregate in
a small open space within the city walls. They brought milk,
cheese and other animal and farm products to trade with the
local population and bought their essential needs with the
proceeds. The word 'Manakh', or 'place of seating of the
camels', was used to describe this open space and so it became
known.

After the commencement of oil production and the increasing
wealth it brought to the country, much money was invested
in the creation of local infrastructure, and a prestigious multi-
storied market building, with car parking on several floors, and
shops and office on others, was constructed on the same site.
Towards the end of the 1970s the ground floor of the building
gradually became a focal point for investors and speculators.
They gathered in the pleasant air-conditioned atrium at the
centre of the building for the purpose of transacting business,
and gradually shops and offices around the floor were bought
out and the premises converted into offices for brokers and
others providing attendant services for those engaged in 'the
market', which eventually the floor of the building became. It
was the collapse of the trade in this market which generated
the Kuwait Stock Market crisis of 1982, and gave it its eventual
name, the Al Manakh crisis. The crisis, as we shall see, had
profound effects throughout the state, threatening its economy
and its very foundations. Its containment by the authorities
had to be undertaken judiciously, step by step, and with regard
to the special circumstances of the times and Kuwait's socio-

economic structure. It also had to be undertaken within the confines of the local banking and commercial system, which itself had been developed as part of that same structure. It is to the examination of the way in which the crisis was contained, and the evaluation of the repercussions which later arose, that this chapter is addressed, but in order to put the examination and analysis in context, a description of how a number of the major financial institutions and authorities in Kuwait came into being and were later developed may assist readers in understanding what follows.

THE STOCK MARKET – THE EARLY DAYS

The Kuwait Stock Market dates back to the formation of the first Kuwait shareholding company, the National Bank of Kuwait, in 1952. This was followed in 1954 by the National Cinema Company, but by 1979 the total number of Kuwaiti shareholding companies had only reached 43. Furthermore, four of these were later taken over by the Government, namely the Kuwait National Petroleum Company, the Kuwait Petrochemical Industries Company, the Kuwait Oil Tankers Company and the Kuwait Transport Company.

The first law governing 'financial papers' in the country was promulgated in 1962, but this was intended to regulate dealings in foreign financial papers as local papers were still comparatively negligible in number. It was not until the start of the 1970s that the volume of local papers began to grow rapidly, and it soon became evident that new rules and regulations were necessary to regulate the local market. Accordingly Law 32 of 1970 gave the Minister of Commerce and Industry the authority to make resolutions necessary for regulating trade in financial papers relating to Kuwaiti shareholding companies. A financial consultative committee was set up with the Minister of Commerce and Industry as chairman, two further representatives from his Ministry, one each from the Ministry of Finance and the Central Bank, and five citizens with experience in this field. The committee was required to:

1 Propose legal provisions and organisation measures relating to the Stock Market.
2 Draw up proposals to establish a Stock Exchange.

3 Propose laws to preserve the country's economic and financial interests in the light of extraordinary fluctuations in the
prices of financial papers.
4 Give opinions and advice on the registration of foreign
financial papers in Kuwait.

The Stock Exchange had a very informal beginning. It started
life in the basement of an old building in the City's souk, or
market area. Although it had been established on 31 October
1962, as mentioned above, there was practically no local market
for shares. It was not until 26 November 1970 that the official
Stock Market received formal legal recognition.

On the first day of its opening shares worth KD 21 million
were reported as having been traded. These were all in the 22
Kuwaiti companies registered up to that date. It was not until
1973 that official statistics were published on the volume and
price of stock dealt on the exchange, but by 1977 trading had

Table 2.1 Number of quoted Kuwait shareholding companies

Sector	1970	1976	1979	1984
Banks	4	6	8	8
Insurance	3	3	4	4
Investment Co.	2	3	3	4
Industrial Co.	7	10	13	13
Transport co.	2	2	5	6
Services Co.	4	4	4	6
Real estate Co.	–	3	3	3
Total	22	31	40	44

Source: Central Bank of Kuwait, Statistical Bulletins.

Table 2.2 Value of stock traded (in thousand dinars)

Sector	1976–9 (annual average)	1980–88 (annual average)
Banks	159,427	124,669
Insurance	5,034	8,197
Investment Co.	134,208	103,144
Industrial Co.	129,649	110,530
Transport Co.	56,644	70,295
Services Co.	13,954	72,909
Real estate	79,901	146,053
Total	578,817	635,797

Source: Central Bank of Kuwait, Statistical Bulletins.

grown significantly, reaching KD 9,533 million in 38 companies (see Tables 2.1 and 2.2).

The prime aim of the Government was to encourage entrepreneurship and to promote investment in Kuwait's development and in diversification of the Kuwait economy, especially in light manufacture. It had been actively encouraging the private sector for many years, notably by injecting purchasing power into the economy and making investment funds available to the general public. This was being accomplished by cheap loans, Government land distribution and purchase and provision of free services. These disbursements had been criticised by a series of World Bank missions to the country between 1961 and 1965 on the grounds that such injections only encouraged capital outflow due to the comparative lack of opportunity for investment in the domestic economy. Hence the authorities deliberately used the Stock Exchange as part of its package of incentives to encourage the private sector to keep its money in the country and invest in those economic activities which would contribute to national development.

The growth of the Stock Market was inexorably linked with the sharply rising flows of funds into the domestic economy after the Tehran Oil Agreement of 1971. Unlike other major financial centres, however, certain features of the Kuwaiti Stock Market rendered the Kuwaiti situation probably unique. Elsewhere, stock exchanges grew as means for the efficient gathering of scarce funds for investment in new or expanding enterprises. In Kuwait the reverse was the case. Compared with Government injections of capital into the private sector the opportunities for the direct investment of this capital were very limited. The main vehicles for investment were existing shares or real estate. When an entrepreneur decided to tap the market for funds to support a new venture the issue was invariably tremendously over-subscribed. The inevitable consequences of this constant excess of demand over supply resulted in gross inflation of share prices and over-speculation. Thus, instead of the capital market being a secondary market offering liquidity to investors and long-term finance to companies, from its beginnings its development has mainly been in response to speculative forces.

At first, the dynamism of the speculative market was provided by the enormous increase in oil exports which in turn

generated the high levels of Government expenditure in infrastructure and public services and also by direct injections as
part of the national policy of spreading wealth among the
people. Unfortunately, this strong inflow of private liquidity
was further augmented by a parallel system of post-dated
cheques. Although Government injections were already vast,
they were in the ultimate limited. But the use of post-dated
cheques on a large scale removed all limits on credit creation
completely. Furthermore, it was a practice outside the control
of the normal banking system. The inevitable abuse which the
availability of such credit generated resulted in equally inevitable crises, notably the crisis of 1977, but above all the great
Manakh crash of 1982. How the post-dated cheque system
operated will be detailed later, but a short description of the
1977 crisis and the Governmental response to it will serve to
illustrate how Kuwait had been feeling its way forward into
new territory under conditions for which there were no previous experiences to provide adequate guidance.

THE 1977 CRISIS

The increases in the national oil revenues and subsequent
increases in private liquidity dating from the early 1970s, as
illustrated above, caused a large increase in actvity in the Stock
Market. The total value of transactions in 1976 was 134 per

Table 2.3 Kuwaiti shareholding companies, volume of traded stocks,
and prices

Sector	1976			1977		
	Share quantity (value)	Share volume (1,000s)	Change in price (%)	Share quantity (value)	Share volume (1,000s)	Change in price (%)
Banks	7,802,335	83,261	121.9+	2,422,660	26,461	12.1−
Investment	50,008,420	267,641	176.2+	15,282,142	87,896	29.7−
Insurance	675,265	10,209	201.1+	178,648	3,098	7.3−
Industrial	63,991,466	208,146	124.4+	15,978,738	77,115	23 −
Transport	23,419,326	136,959	49.5+	18,684,917	79,202	18.3−
Services	650,357	6,716	143.6+	71,500	667	4.8−
Real estate	28,894,400	232,935	238.1+	6,951,940	71,238	21.6−
Total	175,441,569	945,867	134.7+*	59,570,545	345,677	18.7−*

Source: Central Bank of Kuwait, Annual Reports.
* Average, weighted by volume in each sector.

19

cent greater than that of 1975. Further, much of this increase had been generated by forward transactions so that a fall in prices was inevitable. This took place in early 1977 and Table 2.3 shows how prices collapsed and, even more so, how the volume of activity on the market plummeted.

Prior to the collapse, and noting the unhealthy trend in share prices, the Ministry of Commerce and Industry issued in November 1976 its Resolution No. 61, concerning trade in financial papers of Kuwaiti shareholding companies. A 'Committee of Securities' was set up under this Resolution and was given wide powers to regulate dealings in the securities market. The committee was requested to:

1 Draw up a series of organisational rules for trading in securities. These rules to cover methods and procedures, registration, cash and forward transactions, determination of brokerage practices and fees, hours of trading, etc.
2 To investigate complaints relevant to the working of the market. But, before the committee could get into its stride, the collapse of prices had already set in. This led the Ministry of Commerce and Industry to introduce a series of measures:
   (i) The suspension of the establishment of further public shareholding companies. From the date of the Resolution until the first half of 1979 only one public shareholding company was established, the General Storage Company, set up in June 1979.
   (ii) The prohibition of any increase in the capital of existing companies except within limits already permitted. As a result, no company applied for permission to issue new capital throughout 1978. The only increases in capital were achieved through bonus issues.
   (iii) The purchase by the Kuwait Foreign Trading Contracting and Investment Company, on behalf of the Government, of any privately owned shares at fixed floor prices. These prices were based on a formula derived from the prices of the same shares during the previous year. This had the effect of insuring speculators against unlimited falls in the prices of shares in which they were trading. Such purchases continued from December 1977 to April 1978, and amounted to around KD 150 million.

The Government also issued other important resolutions and

directives through agencies such as the Central Bank. These included:

1 Control of credit facilities with a view to directing the flow of credit to desirable sectors.
2 Reduction of interest rates charged by banks to their customers by around 2 per cent, with the shortfall to the banks being made up by a Government subsidy.
3 Extension of existing repayment periods for investors by two years.

The Government's outlay on share purchase of KD 150 million referred to was quite modest compared with its oil revenues at the time of KD 20 million a day (oil production was averaging 2 million barrels per day at a price of $35, or KD 10, per barrel). A week's revenue to support the market seemed a small sacrifice when it is remembered that the Government still held the shares bought, and its expenditure on social services and infrastructural developments at the time were unable to absorb all the Governmental income so that large sums were being directed abroad for investment elsewhere. By contrast, the coming Al Manakh crisis was to absorb over KD 2 billion at a time (1983) when oil production was around 1 million barrels per day and its price $18, or KD 5, per barrel, producing an average daily revenue of KD 5 million only.

THE STOCK MARKET AND THE BANKING SYSTEM

While the Stock Market troubles affected individual investors directly, and Government intervention described so far was equally direct, there were inevitably important repercussions on the banking system, which also played an important role as a medium for the execution of national policy in the troubled periods under review. It is instructive, therefore, to examine the role of the banking system in the economy and to assess its relationship with the various crises which occurred.

The Central Bank

When it was decided, early in the 1960s, that Kuwait should have its own national currency, it was natural that the question of the appropriate machinery for its issue should also be considered. At that time it was felt that a currency board would be more appropriate to the country's immediate needs than a Central Bank, but studies were constantly being made, and their results assessed, during the following years and efforts toward the creation of a Central Bank continued. On 1 April 1969, in accordance with Law 32 of 1968 and a subsequent Amiri Decree of 16 March 1969, the Central Bank of Kuwait was brought into being.

During the initial phase of its existence, the Bank's operations were limited to the issue and redemption of currency, but at the same time it was making preliminary arrangements for the future development of its functions as a fully fledged national institution. Following an Amiri Decree which took effect from 15 November 1969, the Central Bank took the initial steps toward control over the country's commercial banking system. This control needed to be introduced gradually, as until then the commercial banks had not been subject to any central control, nor were detailed data and statistics available on their activities.

It commenced developing its control over the banks by registering them in accordance with regulations issued by the Ministry of Finance. It also commenced collecting appropriate statistical information and other data from the banks according to a specially designed format which would facilitate its future activities in the regulation of the country's banking system. It should be remembered that the formation of the Central Bank occurred only four years prior to the start of the oil boom years when Government income and consequent injections into the domestic economy began to escalate. The tremendous cash flows commenced when the Bank was still in an early stage of development. Yet, from the outset, its controlling authorities were very much aware of the dangers that could arise from large increases in liquidity in the face of comparatively restricted opportunities for investment. In 1974 it imposed a liquidity ratio of 25 per cent on the banks, altering this to a graded system in 1978. Simultaneously it tried to control the direction of lending by instituting a system of reporting on the distribution of loans among the main divisions of the economy, and by establishing an informal system of reporting on individuals' indebtedness to various banks. In the comparatively informal environment which characterised Kuwait's commercial life it was extremely difficult to control the direction of credit, and aggressive control measures like imposition of high liquidity ratios met with only limited success.

The authorities had started compiling statistics on the composition of domestic credit by the end of 1972. During the late 1970s it was found that 50 per cent of total bank lending was for the personal and the financial services sectors. The remainder was for 'productive' lending to the commercial sectors. This obviously meant that banks had either directly, or indirectly through local finance companies, provided substantial funds for speculative investment. This is all the more evident when comparing the later figures with those for the beginning of the reporting period, when credit to trade absorbed over 30 per cent, agriculture 5 per cent, fisheries 5 per cent and construction 20 per cent. Only 40 per cent went to the personal and financial sectors. Thus, loan demand would appear to have been a large contributory factor in the creation of liquidity as the 1970s progressed, in spite of the attempts by the Central Bank to siphon off excess liquidity, and the Government's reduction in the levels of land purchase which undoubtedly stemmed some of the inflow of cash into the system. But how far was the credit created through the banking system responsible for the expanding bubble which eventually burst?

On deeper analysis, it is obvious that even if easy credit initiated the speculative fever, it was the exploitation of loopholes in the legal framework of stock market regulations and the creation of a parallel credit system based on post-dated cheques that were the prime bases for the speculative frenzy which was to end in disaster. It is to this parallel system, devoid of any regulation, therefore, that we must turn for further elucidation of the causes of the crises under discussion.

Forward contracts and post-dated cheques

The main method used for speculation during the boom years 1976 to early 1982 was the forward contract. Under such a contract, two dealers would strike a forward deal at an agreed price, which would include a premium over the spot price. In 1976, this premium was 20–30 per cent per annum; already high, but by the end of 1981 and the beginning of 1982 it had reached anything between 200 per cent or sometimes even 500 per cent.

A forward contract of stock purchase was invalid in Kuwaiti law, but the market found an easy way around this by using post-dated cheques for payment on delivery. This was possible because a valid action could be brought on the cheques even if the underlying contract was unenforceable. Consequently, a cheque, albeit post-dated, was a guarantee of payment. However, like forward contracts, Kuwaiti law does not recognise post-dating of cheques, so that the receiver of a cheque could in theory present it at any time during the currency of the contract. So, present delivery of the share became a precondition of the forward contract.

Early in 1977 an attempt was made by the Ministry of Commerce to impose on the market a regulated system of forward dealing. Such deals were permitted for periods of up to twelve months' duration, and were to be registered at the Ministry's Department of Securities. The buyer was required to pay the premium element at once and the balance on maturity, but he would not receive the shares until payment was complete. This system was intended to function in a manner close to that of forward dealing on the London Options Market, but with an important distinction. Unlike his counterpart in London, the Kuwaiti dealer could not withdraw from the contract merely by forfeiting the premium. This possibility was purposely avoided by those who drafted the legislation on the grounds that it would encourage trading on pure chance, i.e. gambling on the future value of the underlying shares. This was deemed to be in contravention of Islamic Law.

Although deals under these new procedures were to be enforceable in law, were to be registered, restricted to a maximum of twelve months, and the delivery of shares forbidden until final completion, the intimate and informal nature of the market was such that the new legislation was soon disregarded and traders returned to their old ways of immediate delivery of shares against post-dated cheques for forward payment.

The post-dated cheque and bank credit

Post-dated cheques were often issued by merchants and traders in the commercial section of the market. As such, they formed

24

an essential element in the system of trade credit. These cheques would be discounted by the commercial banks according to their rating of the creditworthiness of the drawers and recipients. Although in law these cheques were legally enforceable at any time, it was normal bank practice to hold them until their indicated dates. In fact, they were treated in much the same way as a trade bill would be treated on the traditional London market. This practice, formerly restricted to trade-related contracts, was gradually extended to Stock Market transactions, and it was difficult for the commercial banks to differentiate between credit obtained in this way for commercial and for speculative purposes. Since most of the trading companies were sole proprietorships or family partnerships, and since there was no legislation requiring such firms to maintain accounts separate from those of the personal accounts of the owners, it was impossible to distinguish between the two types of lending.

There is no doubt that part of the credit which led to the eventual collapse of the market was provided by the banking system, anxious to lend in the face of the high liquidity available to it and the comparatively profitable business which it entailed. But there is equally no doubt that the main source of the flood of credit which took the market to its dizzy heights from which it eventually crashed was the system of forward dealing.

The delivery of a share against a post-dated cheque gave the system an unusual potential for leverage, as the delivery immediately provided collateral for further purchases on the forward market. A broker could sell a share on the spot market and buy it back on the forward market, obtaining cash which could then be lent out on the Stock Market at high rates. He could repeat this transaction a number of times in sequence, using the same shares and each time generating more cash.

It was this type of brokers' credit and credit advanced between major traders in the market, who were able to discount each others' cheques, which together formed the bulk of the credit internally generated by the Stock Market. Furthermore, the original flow need not have come from the banks at all. The banks were drawn into the market as followers not leaders, and although the profits on personal lending were high, the temptation to maximise profits by indulging in lending for speculation was always tempered by the bank management's' natural caution and the Central Bank's limits of tolerance.

The high interest rates which were a continuous temptation to the banks to lend were undoubtedly generated by the system of present delivery of shares against a forward contract of payment, and this generated a vicious upward spiral in premium rates on forward transactions. If the law on forward trading had been heeded, both the 1978 and the later, much larger, Al Manakh crash of 1982 could never have occurred. But, it must be asked, if there was illegal speculation, on what were the operators in the market speculating? The answer lies in another of the pieces of the jigsaw that together made up Al Manakh.

KUWAITI AND GULF SHAREHOLDING COMPANIES

The main objects of speculation in Kuwait during the times leading up to the crisis were shares in what came to be known collectively as Gulf companies. For these to be traded in Kuwait yet another Kuwaiti law had to be circumvented. This was the law on Kuwaiti shareholding companies. As a result of the 1977 crisis, the Government had introduced measures which restricted the licensing of new shareholding companies in order to curb the rapid and largely insecure expansion on the Kuwait Stock Exchange. Also, as in all the major stock markets, shares could not be traded in any registered shareholding company until after its first year's balance sheet and accounts had been audited and published. In order to circumvent these regulations, entrepreneurs wishing to form new ventures registered their companies offshore – generally in Bahrain or the United Arab Emirates. It was shares in these companies, Gulf shares as they came to be known, which were freely traded over the counter in the unofficial market, Al Manakh.

The first of such shares to be traded appeared in 1976. These were of a company based outside Kuwait but within the GCC, and interestingly, when the licence was granted by the Ministry of Commerce, it was assumed that these shares would be governed by the laws relating to Kuwaiti public companies (i.e. no official trading could take place in them until the first annual accounts had been published and, most significantly, that the founders could not sell their shares until three years after the first share issue). This law on the so-called 'closed shareholding companies' was in fact designed specifically to prevent the occurrence of bubbles and their collapse. It was disregard for this law that was later to prove so disastrous.

With the success of this Gulf company issue the founders immediately began to sell their shares, claiming that since the company was registered outside Kuwait, Kuwaiti law did not apply to it. A ban on secondary market trading in these shares was immediately imposed by the Ministry of Commerce and was extended to other companies that were to follow. However, like the law against forward dealing, this ban was universally ignored and Gulf companies began to mushroom from then onward. Details of Gulf companies are shown in Table 2.4.

Table 2.4 The development of new Gulf companies 1970–84

Sector	1970	1976	1977	1978	1979	1980	1981	1982	1983/4	Total
Banking	–	–	–	–	1	2	1	1	–	5
Investment	–	1	–	–	5	1	–	2	–	9
Insurance	1	1	–	1	1	1	1	–	–	6
Real estate	–	–	–	–	2	–	–	2	–	4
Industrial	–	1	3	–	3	5	–	–	–	12
Services	–	2	1	1	1	–	–	–	–	5
Total	1	5	4	2	13	9	2	5	–	41

Source: Central Bank of Kuwait, Statistical Bulletins.
Note: During 1971–75 and 1983–4 no new companies were established.

Further measures were introduced in 1979 in an attempt to curb the growth in Gulf companies by ordering the closure of the Registrar's Office in Kuwait so that no transfers of titles in closed and Gulf companies could be registered. Almost immediately registration of the transfer of titles was being arranged by telex at various companies' head offices, and the unofficial market in Gulf shares hardly faltered.

The Kuwaiti authorities made one last attempt to resolve the situation by issuing guidelines for Gulf companies seeking recognition. Briefly, these were that a company should have been in existence for at least three years, should have a capital of at least KD 5 million, and all its shares should be owned by citizens of Gulf Co-operation Council states (i.e. Kuwait, Bahrain, Saudi Arabia, Qatar, Oman and the United Arab Emirates), with at least half of the shares being Kuwaiti owned. Most importantly, the authorities stipulated that a company's objectives were to be clearly defined and it must be able to show a profit of at least 10 per cent on its capital earned according to activities stated in its articles and memorandum of association. Finally, it was required that a company should give an undertaking neither to form any subsidiary nor to seek any fresh capital within at least two years from the grant of listing. It is little wonder that in the face of all these requirements only two Gulf companies, Gulf Real Estate of Ajman and Gulf Agriculture of Sharjah, were listed and traded officially.

3

AL MANAKH

THE RISE OF AL MANAKH

In spite of all the efforts of the public authorities, the formation of Gulf companies went on unabated. Around 32 companies were formed between 1978 and 1981. Each issue was 'an overwhelming success', in that when the shares were offered to the Kuwaiti public, they were over-subscribed many hundreds of times. They were shares which were also cheap in comparison with officially listed shares.

Most of the issues were handled by banks in Bahrain. An applicant could only apply for a maximum in each issue, generally around 30,000, but some of the leading traders on the Manakh took to employing nominees, often illiterate nomads and villagers from the surrounding areas of Kuwait City. They would obtain their power of attorney and the use of their identity cards in return for a fee, apply for shares on their behalf and then transfer these to their own names after allotment. It was not unknown for such traders to descend on Bahrain with suitcases full of applications obtained in this way, ready to make many hundreds of proxy applications for the maximum permitted number of shares whenever a new issue was about to be opened.

The procedures adopted in the issue and allotment of shares also lent itself to abuse. For example, some of the Gulf companies had their shares denominated in US dollars. Suppose the share price of a new issue to be $1. Applicants would usually be required to pay 5 cents only on application. By the rules of the Bahrain Monetary Agency this was required to be from the applicant's own funds. But there was no way in which the bank handling the application could verify that this was so, as an applicant could always cover the amount due with an overdraft on another bank. The balance of 95 cents to be paid would then be treated as a loan and the total $1 transferred by the bank to the issue account of the new company. The list of applicants would then be forwarded to the registrars of the issue; usually a locally incorporated firm of chartered accountants. These would finalise the allotment within two weeks and return the list to the bank. As these issues were invariably grossly oversubscribed the individual allotment would be very meagre. But meantime, the bank having received 5 cents for each share applied for, and making a loan of 95 cents on each, would make a handsome profit on the issue. As these applications were so oversubscribed, the total amounts received on application were always sufficient to cover the interest on the 95 cents per share given as a loan, plus the cost of the shares actually alloted and still leave a residue to be returned to each applicant. The banks were happy, as the profits on these deals were large and in effect guaranteed from the application money already received, and the applicants were happy as they confidently expected the shares allocated to show a substantial profit which could immediately be realised on the unofficial market.

The problems caused by these abuses were exacerbated by another ruse adopted by promoters of Gulf companies. This was to inflate the number of shares by very large increases in companies' nominal capital through rights or bonus issues, often accompanying this increase by share splits. This had the effect of sharply reducing share prices while making more shares available in the market, but creating the illusion that investors were receiving handsome distributions. By May/June 1982 5 billion shares were being traded on the market, and the daily volume of transactions reached 14 million a day, with prices often doubling or tripling in a matter of weeks.

Even though it was undoubtedly local conditions which generated and fuelled the euphoric conditions in Al Manakh, world conditions did not help. As shown in previous pages, the sharp increase in oil prices in 1979/80 had created a vast increase in Government receipts in all the main oil-producing countries, resulting in increased Government expenditure and consequent domestic liquidity (see Table 3.1). But whereas the industrial powers in 1973 and the following years tried to combat the problem of the price rises of those years by encouraging the recycling of 'petrodollars' and thus keeping world interest rates low, they changed their approach to the rises of 1979–80, taking a monetarist stance and raising interest rates sharply, causing recessionary conditions, and hoped to counter the outflow of funds by reducing imports. The enormous increase in liquidity in Kuwait and other Gulf countries coincided with a reduction in investment opportunities abroad.

Table 3.1 Government revenue and expenditure 1974–84

Year	Total spending[1]	Oil revenue[2]	Notes
1974	621.3	3020	
1975–6	794.9	2956.6	
1976–7	1172.9	2519.7	First crisis
1977–8	1745.5	2575.3	Weakening of the market
1978–9	1749.9	5940.5	
1979–80	2210.7	4417.0	
1980–1	3115.8	5059.2	Peak of the market
1981–2	3538.2	4117.8	Second crisis (and Manakh)
1982–3	3501.3	2805.5	
1983–4	3475.3	3080.3	

1 and 2 *Source*: Reports of the Central Bank of Kuwait.

Also, the Iran–Iraq war had originally caused investors to shy away from the official stock market in Kuwait but by 1981 their fears had subsided somewhat, although long-term investments may well have still appeared somewhat risky. The short-term gains on a rising, if unofficial, market must therefore

Table 3.2 The annual percentage changes of liquidity

Year	Percentage change of liquidity over previous year	Notes
1979	+17.6	
1980	+24.8	
1981	+35.4	The climax
1982	− 8.0	The crisis
1983	+ 4.5	
1984	+ 3.0	

Source: Reports of the Central Bank of Kuwait.

have appeared very tempting indeed, especially after the Kuwaiti Government increased its domestic expenditure by 40 per cent in 1981, an action which increased domestic liquidity by a further 35 per cent over the previous year (see Table 3.2).

As well as Kuwaiti speculators, the Manakh market had a special attraction for non-Kuwaitis, as these latter were denied direct access to the official Kuwaiti Stock Exchange. Soon 'investors' were flocking to Al Manakh from all sections of society and all walks of life. Salaried employees, university students, housewives, taxi-drivers, all seeking the quick profits which Al Manakh seemed to offer, joined the Manakh bandwagon. Kuwaiti contractors were even underbidding on construction contracts, confident that even though their receipts would not cover costs, they would be able to make up the difference on the Manakh market, where prices seemed to be endlessly soaring.

However, profits are never realised until cash is received, and forward dealing had become the standard method of trading and the post-dated cheque the method of payment. Furthermore, most of the Gulf companies only existed on paper, operating at accommodation addresses, such as care of hotel suites. For example, one company, the Kuwaiti Tyres Company, did not produce a single tyre. Many were also formed for the sole purpose of speculating in real estate and shares, which effectively meant ploughing receipts back into Al Manakh. Some were even floated merely to provide shares for the ever-hungry market, with the founders deftly pocketing the difference between the issue price and the market price. These practices soon led to a differential opening between the premium rates for shares on the official and unofficial markets. Early in 1981 the quoted share premium on the official exchange was 12/15 per cent, while on Gulf shares on Al Manakh it was 40/50 per cent. Experienced operators seized the opportunity to arbitrage between the two markets, forcing up both forward and premium rates and prices. By the end of 1981 Gulf share prices had risen by 200 per cent, and official Boursa shares by 50 per cent.

The continuation of such a financial merry-go-round, like all others of its type before, was dependent upon an ever-increasing flow of new funds in order to keep spot prices moving. But every merry-go-round has to stop at some time and any stock market boom not based upon rising corporate earnings carries within itself the seeds of its own destruction. In October 1981 a conference on stock markets was organised by the Kuwait Chamber of Commerce and Industry. Prominent local and foreign speakers warned of the dangers and the inevitable disaster that the unregulated speculative fever would bring. Yet the Manakh market scarcely paused for breath, as the warnings were not backed by any signs that the Government intended to intervene. The Ministry of Commerce and Industry still adhered to its long-held view that the Manakh was illegal and, therefore, the Government could not be held responsible for regulating any trade conducted there.

THE FINAL CRASH

From the spring of 1982 all the ingredients of a crash were becoming evident. In their efforts to obtain liquidity traders raised forward premiums to even further record heights. But at the same time, share prices on both the Boursa and Al Manakh began a slow slide downwards. This immediately began to put pressure on some of the major dealers in the Manakh. Many post-dated cheques were becoming due, and the drawers found themselves short of liquidity at the same time as the depression in the share prices was lowering the value of their portfolios. In early May the documented record of open forward positions in the official market showed an aggregate of KD 4.5 billion, with settlement dates stretching over three years. To cover these positions, spot prices needed to be doubled by December 1982, and doubled again by May 1983. The situation in the Manakh was much worse, with the size of the positions and the needed earnings to cover the premiums being much greater.

Beginning from mid-May 1982 the market index fell steadily from 600 to just below 500 in mid-August. But in July–August the first of a very large tranche of forward positions, entered into twelve months previously, were becoming due. The situation was temporarily alleviated in July when some of the larger dealers entered into mutual off-setting agreements to cover one month's commitments. However, the end of Ramadan was approaching and a major dealer who had cheques falling due to him during the five days' holiday which commences at the end of the twenty-eight days' fast presented the cheques before the holiday and not after it. This precipitated the collapse and the market tumbled like the proverbial house of cards.

Due to the informal nature of the market and the Government's previous insistence that it could not be responsible for the regulation of a market which was not established within the law, there was none of the record-keeping that would normally be expected in other markets. The size of the overall debt, the list of debtors and creditors (a great many people were both), and the maturities and premium of the forward transactions were all unrecorded. There was not even a formal market clearing system in being.

THE GOVERNMENT ACTS

When the Government finally intervened, it did so fast. It had first to establish a complete register of the debtors and creditors and the exact nature of the debts owed and owing to each. In the words of the then Minister of Finance, 'It was necessary to separate the crisis from the rest of the economy and to protect the value of the national currency.' The register was set up within days, the Government establishing a very early deadline for registration, after which unregistered claims would not be deemed valid. The Chamber of Commerce quickly proposed that all forward debts be settled with a maximum premium of 20 per cent over face value, but this did not meet with favour at the individual or the national level.

It was realised that the crisis was of a size which could shake the commercial sector of the economy to its foundations and that Government policy had to be formulated in such a way that its own intervention at any point in the network of debt did not precipitate a disastrous chain reaction. It first set up a Fund for Small Investors and Creditors. This had an initial capital of KD 500 million (US$ 1.75 billion). A small investor was deemed one owed not more than KD 2 million, admittedly an amazingly high figure by the standards of any other society, but small in relation to the problem in hand at the time, as ensuing paragraphs will show.

Cash payments from the fund were to be paid immediately to those owed KD 100,000 or less, and the remainder were to receive a similar cash payment but the remainder, up to the KD 2 million ceiling, were to be paid in guaranteed Government bonds according to the following schedule:

Value of transaction		bond maturity
KD 100,001 to KD	250,000	6 months
250,001	500,000	12 months
500,001	750,000	3 years
750,000	1,000,000	4/5 years

By registering with the fund the creditor was considered to have surrendered in full his rights to debts in respect of unsettled transactions in excess of KD 2 million in total. The fund charged a fee of 1 per cent of the value of each case registered. At the same time, the Government was urging that as many as possible of those affected should come to some arrangement with their debtors and creditors on an independent basis.

It was not made clear initially whether the bonds issued by the fund could be discounted through the banking system, but the matter was clarified later when the Government permitted the commercial banks to discount these bonds at 7.5 per cent per annum and to re-discount them with the Central Bank at 7.25 per cent. Furthermore, these bonds could be held in the banks' portfolios and considered as liquid assets and regarded as part of the banks' liquidity requirements.

The Government made it clear that at the time of announcing the fund it did not intend to order any general scaling down of debts. Those who could not meet their liabilities and could not come to an arrangement with their creditors would be allowed to go to the wall. In particular, the Government was offering no compensation or assistance to those owing more than KD 2 million.

THE KUWAIT CLEARING COMPANY

On 20 September 1982, the rights of citizens to payment on maturity of post-dated cheques was temporarily suspended (Amiri Decree 57, 1982). A closed shareholding company, the Kuwait Clearing Company, was formed with a capital of KD 6.5 million. The shareholders were the seven commercial banks, the two specialised banks, the three 'K's (the Kuwait Investment Company, Kuwait International Investment Company, Kuwait

Foreign Trading, Contracting and Investment Company), and the Public Institution for Social Security. The decree required the registration of all post-dated cheques with the Clearing Company, together with proof of the underlying transactions within a period of one month. The total of cheques registered was 28,878 and the total of individuals involved was in excess of 6,000. The total value of the cheques was KD 26.7 billion (US$ 90 billion). Of this, KD 18.5 billion worth had been drawn by just eight individuals, the so-called Cavaliers of Al Manakh. A breakdown of the cheques registered is shown in Table 3.3.

Table 3.3 Post-dated cheques registered with the Clearing Company and their maturity dates

Major speculators	
8 individuals, approx. total exposure	KD 18.00 billion
Middle investors	
Approx. 500 individuals, approx. total exposure	KD 7.00 billion
Small investors	
Approx. 5,500 individuals, approx. total exposure	KD 2.00 billion
Total Value (approx.)	*year of maturity*
KD 11 billion	1982
KD 14 billion	1983
KD 1.7 billion	1984

ARBITRATION COMMITTEE

Immediately following the setting up of the Clearing Company, an Arbitration Committee was established (Amiri Decree 59). This was to have jurisdiction over all disputes concerning forward share dealing. It was vested with powers to ban individuals from disposing of assets or travelling abroad. It had powers to investigate and arbitrate on all cases referred to it by the registration authority, and in its adjudications it was not necessarily bound by the provisions of existing civil and criminal law. It could order payment by instalments if deemed appropriate, cancel debts it believed to be fictitious, nullify a contract or adjust the amount of a forward contract to its spot price at the relevant date plus a percentage to be laid down by the Council of Ministers.

On any dispute referred to it the Committee could stay all civil, commercial and criminal proceedings pertaining to the relevant transactions and their method of payment, including proceedings for declaration of bankruptcy. If the Committee deemed that a debtor's financial condition had deteriorated to the point where his assets were unlikely to cover his liabilities, then they could refer the individual's case to the Public Prosecutor with a view to initiating bankruptcy proceedings.

If the Committee found that a debtor had transferred assets abroad, or had assigned them to others in a way that was detrimental to the interests of his creditors, then they could order that the assets be brought back within the Committee's jurisdiction by a specified date. Non-compliance could incur a penalty of up to five years' imprisonment without prejudice to any other penalties laid down by law, and the subject would also be debarred from travelling abroad for fifteen years after his sentence was served. To do so would be regarded as a separate offence subject to a further sentence of five years' imprisonment. These were harsh measures indeed, but it must be recorded that very few Kuwaitis were jailed, or compelled to bring their assets back from abroad, under any orders issued by this Committee.

The decree stipulated that the Committee was to be set up for a maximum of two years only and would automatically be wound up if its work was completed earlier. It also provided that parties to any dealings subject to the Committee's scrutiny could reach amicable settlements among themselves, provided that such settlements did not prejudice the rights of third parties and were submitted to the Committee for approval and enforcement. The Committee was assisted in its work by an Investigating Committee which was empowered to gather information and data for subsequent submission to the Arbitration Committee for its consideration.

THE STORM IN PARLIAMENT

Decree 59 setting up the Arbitration Committee was submitted to the National Assembly as soon as the latter assembled after the summer recess of 1982. Operations under certain provisions of the decree, such as the registration of cheques, had already been commenced, but bitter attacks were launched in the Assembly on the Government for letting matters get so out of hand. There was also strong criticism of the proposal to scale down liabilities, as it was claimed that this would favour the large operators and be to the detriment of the small investor, and that many debtors who were in a position to meet their debts were holding back in the hope that their liabilities would be reduced.

By the time the Assembly resumed its business a week later, however, the Arbitration Committee had already named the eight large dealers responsible for the main part of the total debt and had banned them from travelling abroad or disposing of any of their assets. The eight did, in fact, include a member of the National Assembly, and this led to acrimonious exchanges on the floor of the Assembly as to whether failure to give prior notice of this matter was a breach of Parliamentary privilege. Such altercations further impeded resolution of the main issues.

GOVERNMENT SUPPORT TO THE BOURSA AND THE BANKS

In spite of its initial refusal to contemplate financial support for any rescue strategy, the Government eventually relented and in October 1983 commenced supporting the official Stock Market. By mid-November it had spent more than KD 250 million in the purchase of shares. This it did by buying small lots of not more than 5,000 shares in any one deal from small investors at fixed prices. These purchases were usually made through Government intermediaries (mainly the Kuwait Foreign Trading, Contracting and Investment Company). They were restricted to Boursa shares only and no purchases were permitted of Manakh shares. In spite of these measures, the volume and value of traded shares still declined drastically (Table 3.4). In addition, the Government deposited KD 100 million with the banks in September to help ease their liquidity shortage and by December had added a further KD 97 million to this figure.

THE ESTABLISHMENT FOR THE SETTLEMENT OF FORWARD SHARE TRANSACTIONS

As the crisis wore on, a particular danger to the whole of the commercial community was becoming apparent. Under

Table 3.4 Quantities and values of Kuwaiti shareholding companies traded, 1981–5 (figures in millions)

Sector	1981		1982		1983		1984		1985	
	Shares qty	Value KD	Shares qty	Value KD	Shares qty	Value KD	Shares qty	Value KD	Shares qty	Value KD
Banks	30.5	518	33.6	668	12.9	183	8.4	69	18.9	83.0
Investment	42.8	309	25.6	196	10.2	60	1.3	5	0.8	0.86
Insurance Co.	1.4	23	3.9	76	1.8	29	0.1	1	0.2	0.6
Industrial	40.5	139	39.0	167	16.2	67	2.3	7	5.9	8.0
Transport Co.	34.0	198	9.4	60	3.3	13	0.4	1	1.3	2.9
Services Co.	47.8	127	10.6	64	5.1	18	2.8	2	11.2	7.08
Real estate Co.	49.8	640	61.8	629	11.9	110	4.5	27	3.8	9.0
	246.8	1954	183.9	1860	61.4	480	19.8	112	42.1	111.44

Source: Central Bank of Kuwait Statistical Bulletins.

39

Kuwait's commercial law, it was mandatory that all debts owed to a person declared bankrupt be called in immediately. This held the prospect referred to earlier, that a chain of bankruptcies could be caused as one person defaulting on debts to another could force the latter into insolvency, who in turn would be forced to default on debts to another, and so on. To meet this problem, a further decree, number 75 of 1983, was passed in April of that year. This set up a Government institution that would in effect act as a trustee in bankruptcy. This was an independent entity attached to the Ministry of Finance and was called the 'Establishment for the Settlement of Forward Share Transactions', or 'The Establishment', for short. It was given the following objectives:

1 To assist in establishing means for creditors of anyone declared bankrupt to meet their debts and thus obviate the possibility that the long wait by creditors for the distribution of a bankrupt's assets could result in their own bankruptcy.
2 Making a Dinar evaluation of a bankrupt's assets prior to a declaration of bankruptcy.
3 Expediting bankruptcy proceedings to permit their finalisation as quickly as possible.
4 Investigating ways of reducing the number of bankruptcies to a minimum.
5 Overseeing the sale of a bankrupt's property and other assets in such a way that the harm to the local economy would be minimised.

In order to achieve these objectives, the Establishment was charged with the following tasks:

1 As far as possible to arrange the amicable settlement of transactions concluded in accordance with Decree 57 of 1982 (this decree set up the Kuwait Clearing Company for post-dated cheques and urged that as far as possible debts should be settled by mutual agreement). If such settlements were agreeable to creditors owed 75 per cent of a debtor's total debts, then the settlement was ruled to be effective for the remaining 25 per cent also.
2 Administering, liquidating, controlling and implementing such settlements and accords in accordance with the law.
3 Issuing bonds for the assessed value expected from the reali-

sation of an amicable settlement, from the results of a bankruptcy declaration, or as the result of an interim report on the financial status of a debtor.

In 1984 the Establishment began making payments to creditors in accordance with these assessments. Payment was partly in cash, with the balance in the form of participation bonds. The values of these bonds were based on the settlement amount arrived at after the reduction in premium in accordance with Law 100 of 1983, discussed below.

THE MAIN ISSUE – THE REDUCTION IN PREMIUM

Up to this point all Government measures had failed to address the basic problem – the inordinate size of the premium built into the post-dated cheques. It was these premiums that made the debts of most debtors so large that they could not be covered by their assets. All voluntary efforts to arrange across-the-board reductions, such as those led by the Ministry of Commerce and Industry, had failed. Everyone was waiting for the Government to act.

The Government responded through Law 100 of August 1983, which required premiums to be reduced to between zero and 25 per cent of the spot value of the shares at the time the deal was struck. It was the introduction of this law which precipitated the resignation of the then Finance Minister, Mr Abdlatif Al Hamad, who felt that it unduly favoured defaulters who had precipitated the crisis, and would thus damage Kuwait's reputation in the financial world (it should be noted that when the crisis first broke the value of the Kuwaiti Dinar in the world's markets hardly wavered, surely one of the biggest expressions of confidence in Kuwait's financial integrity that it was possible to make).

The new Finance Minister, Sheikh Khalifa, was equally aware of the dangers of allowing defaulters to escape the consequences of their actions, but in his words, 'Even though in my opinion some people deserve punishment, I cannot have 50 per cent of the business community and private investors going bankrupt and so start a chain reaction affecting the whole economy.'

As a result of all these measures, the actual debt was reduced to an amount far lower than the original total calculated at the commencement of the crisis. Of the original KD 26.7 billion, KD 7.5 billion was settled by negotiations outside the Arbitration Committee. A further KD 7.2 billion was effectively cancelled by Law 100 of 1983, and KD 11.0 billion was effectively cancelled by the cross-clearing of cheques between debtors and also by the Dinar evaluation of debts by the Establishment for the Settlement of Forward Share Transactions. Thus, by the end of 1984, after two years of politically and emotionally charged negotiations, the residual indebtedness had been reduced considerably (see Table 3.5).

Table 3.5 The amount of value of post-dated cheques after revaluation under Law 100/83

Description	Total cheques	The 'real' value of cheques	Value after application of Law 100/83	Cheques value after clearing and Dinar valuation
1 Debts of referred persons on referred persons	6,545	10,946,324	6,175,417	Zero
2 Debts of referred persons on non-referred persons	1,505	1,696,983	875,455	320,000
3 Debts of non-referred persons on referred persons[1]	3,727	4,923,642	3,946,965	470,775
4 Debts of the guarantees fund on referred persons	7,013	1,654,689	1,015,794	264,106
Total	18,790	19,221,638	12,013,631	1,054,881

[1] Decree No. 57/82 had already established a fund with a capital of KD 500 million for the guarantee of the rights of investors.
Source: Haider Hassan Al Jumah, *The Kuwaiti Stock Market Crisis*, Kuwait, Commercial Press, 1986.

In the meantime, the Establishment for the Settlement of Forward Share Transactions had begun reimbursing creditors, but only after each debt had been valued and the outstanding debt reduced in accordance wih Law 100 of 1983 (see above). The reductions varied, but the average valuation was 265 fils for every Dinar of debts referred (1 Kuwaiti Dinar = 1,000 fils). This was somewhat higher than the provisional estimate of 249 fils announced in October 1983.

The disbursements by the Establishment were made through a four-tranche bond issue, as follows:

1 The first tranche corresponded to the holder's pro-rata share in the Establishment's KD 180 million cash pool.
2 The second tranche represented real estate assets.
3 The third tranche represented claims on referred persons.
4 The fourth tranche represented an entitlement by the holder to a pro-rata share in a new investment company in which was vested the referred portfolio of Gulf and Kuwaiti closed shareholding companies which had been the basis of the trade on Al Manakh.

This referred portfolio was administered on behalf of the Establishment by the Kuwait Investment Authority.

The following is a hypothetical example of a creditor owed KD 8,600,000 before the application of Law 100 of 1983, and the payment he might subsequently receive:

Investor 'I' had post-dated cheques totalling KD 8,600,000 before Law 100 1983 and before evaluation.

1 Real Value of post-dated cheques		KD 8,600,000
2 Value after Law 100/83		KD 2,500,000
(The spot value of shares involved at the time deal was struck was	KD 2,000,000	
plus 25 per cent premium allowed	KD 500,000)	
3 Value after referred Dinar valuation		KD 1,500,000
(at 600 fils to the Dinar)		

The payments totalling KD 1,500,000 would be made by the Establishment as follows:

| Description | First tranche | Bond payment | | Date payment | Total payment |
		Second tranche bonds	Third tranche bonds		
1 Cash	100,000				100,000
2 Refund bond		55,000	130,000	15.10.84	185,000
3 Refund bond		55,000	130,000	15.01.85	185,000
4 Refund bond		55,000	130,000	15.04.85	185,000
5 Refund bond		55,000	130,000	15.07.85	185,000
6 Refund bond		–	130,000	15.10.85	130,000
7 Refund bond		–	130,000	15.01.86	130,000
Fourth tranche bonds					1,100,000
Boursa shares fund					400,000
					1,500,000

(*See*: Haider H. Al Jumah, op. cit.)

Thus, the funds committed by the Government directly and indirectly until 1984 were as under:

1 The compensation fund for KD 500 million to compensate small investors up to KD 2 million.
2 A land purchase budget for KD 300 million.
3 Boursa support operations through KFTCIC and KIC around KD 1,000 million.
4 Funds deposited with the banking system in the range of KD 300 million.
5 The loan programmes designed to help investors mortgage property and Boursa shares up to KD 500 million (partly funded by the banks).

The total commitment of the Government through these measures reached around KD 2,500 million.

THE STOCK MARKET AFTER AL MANAKH

All the foregoing Government measures were greeted with great relief and some measure of cautious approval. The injection of liquidity through various measures had encouraged a return of confidence, though at a lower level than previously. However, the measures leave two questions unanswered. The first is the extent to which Government intervention is effective in controlling the market. The second is whether investors have learnt anything at all from the Manakh débacle. These are big questions to which as yet there are no definite answers, but some light on their probabilities will be found in later pages.

NEW STOCK EXCHANGE BUILDING

The establishment of Kuwait Stock Exchange in its new purpose-built building in 1985 portends well for the future of the Stock Market, if only for the way in which it enables controls imposed by the exchange authorities to be made effective. Now all trade is on one floor and is properly registered in order to prevent insider dealing. Post-dated cheques, obviously, are banned. All settlements are to be in cash within three working days of each bargain. The sixteen brokers allowed on the floor have been merged into four brokerage houses, each with a minimum capitalisation of KD 100,000. Each broker has to provide a KD 1 million bank guarantee before being permitted to trade. The Stock Exchange eventually hopes to list around a hundred companies, while Dinar denominated bonds are also being listed, as well as any Government issued debt.

LAWS ENACTED IN 1984

Here it would be appropriate to touch upon important new legal arrangements in the Stock Market during 1984 in the light of the Manakh crisis. The most important of these was Law 42 of 1984, which addressed the following issues. During Al Manakh, the trade in founders' shares conducted by the founders of Gulf companies was taking place before the lapse of the legally specified period. Many of these shares were sold at highly inflated prices, so that after the crash, the purchasers were left holding shares with vastly reduced values. Many of these purchasers later filed civil proceedings, claiming that as the original sales were illegal they should be declared null and void. The situation was complicated further when companies asked the original founders to pay the uncalled share capital instalments, on the grounds that as the subsequent sales were illegal they were still the original founders and shareholders. In practice, the shares had been transferred to new holders who, because of the collapse in prices, had disowned their connections with the companies and refused to pay any further

45

monies due, but the underlying problem was the unlawful transfer 'ab initio'.

The authorities had two choices – either to nullify all such transactions, thus obliging the sellers to refund the amounts paid to them, or to issue a new law retrospectively legitimising them. The latter alternative was adopted, and Law 42 of 1984 was introduced to legalise the trading in Gulf shares. Consequently, those dealers who had attempted to invoke Law 32 of 1970, in order to avoid the losses they had incurred and recover the substantial amount of financial commitments they had borne, were debarred from doing so.

A further decree, issued in August 1984, covered the listing of brokers and their assistants. Each brokerage firm had to be a Kuwaiti joint stock company, with all partners being Kuwaitis. Such partners should not have been declared bankrupt, referred to the Establishment under the regulations covering the Al Manakh crisis, or found guilty of a crime punishable by imprisonment.

TRADING AND PRICES

As anticipated, the volume of trading and the level of prices in the official market declined from 61 million shares (at KD 480 million) in 1983 to 20 million shares (valued at KD 112 million) in 1984 (see Table 3.6).

Furthermore, trading in the second and fourth quarters of the year constituted more than 84 per cent of the year's total. Bank shares ranked first, constituting 42 per cent of total trading, while real estate companies and services companies constituted 23 and 14 per cent respectively. The share price index fell during the year by 48 per cent below the index for 1983. Investment and insurance companies' shares dropped by 59 per cent, while bank and transport companies' shares dropped by 51 and 50 per cent respectively (see Table 3.7). As regards closed shareholding companies listed in the Stock Exchange, the volume and value traded dropped from 12 million shares at KD 33 million in 1983 to just 1.5 million shares at KD 1.6 million in 1984. On the unofficial market, shares of Gulf companies declined in value between 36 and 54 per cent compared with the previous year.

Table 3.6 Kuwaiti shareholding companies volume of traded shares (thousands)

Period	Banks	Investment	Insurance	Shareholding companies		Services	Real estate	Total
				Industrial	Transport			
1978	67,365	43,736	709	26,950	6,340	7,741	20,562	173,403
1979	81,824	24,379	3,452	22,619	8,212	5,530	23,118	169,134
1980	47,686	24,537	1,048	14,833	23,607	9,382	22,616	143,709
1981	30,477	42,778	1,397	40,452	34,027	47,798	49,768	246,697
1982	33,637	25,587	3,902	39,025	9,398	10,641	61,790	183,980
1983	12,868	10,242	1,849	16,221	3,264	5,088	11,879	61,411
1984	8,391	1,289	108	2,345	363	2,794	4,513	19,803

Source: Central Bank of Kuwait, Statistical Bulletins.

Table 3.7 Kuwaiti shareholding companies share price index (1 January, 1987 = 100)

	Banks	Investment	Insurance	Industrial	Transport	Services	Real estate	General index
1976	221.9	276.2	301.1	224.4	149.0	243.6	356.3	235.2
1977	195.1	194.1	579.1	172.7	121.7	231.9	280.1	192.8
1978	315.3	248.1	569.8	226.8	101.2	298.5	384.0	258.9
1979	496.6	258.8	774.9	236.0	113.0	272.5	444.4	311.4
1980	469.7	241.8	693.8	211.9	140.2	359.2	464.5	313.3
1981	729.2	411.7	813.1	297.8	298.1	498.2	793.5	489.6
1982	861.9	470.4	884.6	301.1	324.6	488.0	809.7	509.4
1983	726.5	475.4	811.7	295.8	255.5	411.4	613.4	460.5
1984	353.9	196.0	336.3	172.2	127.7	240.3	373.9	238.6

Source: Central Bank of Kuwait, *The Kuwaiti Economy 1980–4.*
Note: Figures shown for end of each year.

48

4

AL MANAKH AND ITS AFTERMATH

THE COMMERCIAL BANKS

The incipient effects of Al Manakh on the country's commercial banks were obviously enormous, but attempts to analyse the effects of Government intervention, and the measures adopted by the banks themselves, are complicated by the fact that Al Manakh occurred during an era of falling oil prices and general world recession; a recession destined to continue over the following years.

When the collapse occurred in August 1982, and the total value of post-dated cheques was established, hordes of foreign banks immediately descended on Kuwait questioning the Government and bank officials about the solidity of the banking system. Hitherto the reputation of Kuwaiti banks had not been in doubt. Seemingly endless deposits and huge hidden reserves made them the envy of the financial world. But now the Finance Minister found himself having to reassure the press, the public and foreign banks that whatever the outcome of the crisis, the Government was fully behind the banks. In fact, some observers now believe that it was concern for the banking system as a whole that was one of the main reasons for the introduction of Law 100 of 1983, referred to earlier, curtailing premiums to a maximum of 25 per cent.

Yet the banks were not solely or mainly to blame for the reversal of their hitherto impeccable reputation. As already indicated, they were drawn into the Manakh as followers, not leaders. The Manakh was mainly financed by forward contracts and post-dated cheques, which were completely outside the banks' control. The amount of direct involvement of the banks, either through the discounting of post-dated cheques or their acceptance as collateral, was in fact negligible. It totalled only about KD 250 million, or 5 per cent of total bank credit at that time.

THE EFFECT OF AL MANAKH ON BANK ASSETS AND INTEREST RATES

Long before the speculative bubble burst, the Central Bank had been reputedly warning the Kuwaiti banks not to become involved. A directive was issued forbidding banks to accept post-dated cheques or Gulf shares as collateral against loans. An earlier regulation required that in order to be considered fully secure all loans given against shares should have collateral coverage of at least 200 per cent.

Such early steps largely protected the banking system from the full impact of the crisis, but although the direct exposure of banks was minimal, the indirect repercussions on them were manifold. First, a sizeable proportion of credit ostensibly extended for specific productive or commercial purposes found its way into stock market speculation. Monitoring the activities of individuals who were directors in many companies was difficult. Some construction companies tried to make extra profits on contracts by using advance payments for speculation on Al Manakh. New industrial concerns were said to have invested on Al Manakh the advances provided by the Industrial Bank for purchases of materials or investment in development capital. Furthermore, a good part of personal overdraft, which accounted for about one-third of all bank lending, could well have been diverted to the speculation market.

Yet another problem arose from unsecured 'name-lending'. The merchant community in Kuwait is small and inter-related, and a large part of bank credit has been traditionally based on family name and reputation. There are many individuals to whom a request by a bank for a personal balance sheet or an income statement would be considered an affront or offence. But what bankers feared most was the repercussive effect on the second tier of Al Manakh players if any of the top tier were to be declared bankrupt. This second tier comprised around

500 individuals or companies, virtually all of which were customers of the country's banks. What would be the effect on collateral coverage of existing credit facilities? The prices of shares and real estate, in spite of the Government support programme, had already fallen by 50 to 60 per cent over the pre-Manakh days, and banks feared they could find many debtors, previously quite sound, rendered insecure by the actions of others.

The Manakh crisis also had a major effect on local interest rates. Until January 1983, banks were charging up to 10 per cent on KD facilities plus a flat fee of 2 per cent, and giving a maximum 10 per cent on KD deposits. As from February 1983, these rates were reduced by 1 per cent, to 9 per cent plus 2 per cent on loans and 9 per cent on deposits respectively. These were further lowered to 7 per cent plus 2 per cent and 7 per cent respectively from April 1984.

A major reason for the decline in interest rates was the massive injection of liquidity by the Government. Also, the Government made it clear that it did not wish the banks to exert undue pressure on its customers for the repayment of loans during those difficult times. Such uncertainties and the perception of a greatly increased credit risk led to a dramatic shift in lending strategies by the banks. The high growth of the late 1970s and early 1980s in this category of assets gave way to cautious lending on the domestic market and an accelerated push abroad. As one analyst put it, 'The banks have hunkered down to a sort of branch warfare. They have decided to take cover and protect the quality of their assets.'

This siege mentality led to a rapid levelling of asset growth and a contraction in domestic credit. The aggregate assets of the seven commercial banks rose by a meagre 9 per cent to KD 10.0 billion in 1983 while the increase was 20 per cent between 1981 and 1982 (see Table 4.1). Credit extended to the private sector declined in 1983, the first fall in a decade, falling a little more than 1 per cent to KD 3.8 billion against the previous year (see Table 4.2). This is all the more startling when compared with a 30 per cent growth in credit in 1982. The only real domestic credit growth in 1983 was due to the purchase of low yield–low risk Guarantee Fund Bonds issued by the Government on behalf of small investors. Rising to between

Table 4.1 Commercial banks[1] aggregate balance sheet (million dinars)

Items	1981	1982	1983	1984	1985	1986	1987	1988	1989
Total assets	7599.1	9146.2	9994.2	9586.0	9053.2	9307.9	9942.6	10402.0	10972.0
Reserves (cash and balances with Central Bank)	321.6	626.0	372.5	323.0	335.2	288.0	160.9	42.1	38.4
Claims on private sector	3453.6	4292.4	4752.6	5045.4	5067.8	5156.1	5473.2	5659.2	5471.7
Foreign assets	2245.5	2251.0	2301.2	2507.6	2229.6	2179.0	2281.9	2476.4	2839.0
Other assets	1578.4	1976.8	2567.9	1710.0	1420.6	1684.8	2026.6	2224.3	2622.9
Total liabilities	7598.9	9146.3	9994.3	9586.0	9053.3	9307.9	9942.6	10401.9	10972.0
Capital and reserves	411.0	576.9	664.4	823.4	839.9	898.8	1001.9	1031.6	1087.5
Private sector deposits[2]	3583.0	3835.3	4027.1	4171.8	4120.3	4224.7	4435.7	4749.3	4958.8
Government deposits	211.0	393.8	362.5	387.8	385.5	226.6	187.2	93.6	111.7
Foreign liabilities	1264.1	1530.0	1550.4	1560.7	1360.3	1214.0	1205.8	1261.9	1479.6
Other liabilities	2129.8	2810.3	3389.9	2642.3	2347.3	2743.8	3112.0	3265.5	3334.4

[1] National Bank of Kuwait, Commercial Bank of Kuwait, Gulf Bank, Alahli Bank of Kuwait, Bank of Kuwait & Middle East, Burgan Bank, and Bank of Bahrain & Kuwait.

[2] Including certificate of deposits.

Source: Central Bank of Kuwait, *The Economic Report 1988.* Central Bank of Kuwait, *Economic Chart & Statistical Tables 1986* (vol. 8). Figures for 1990 not compiled due to Iraqi occupation.

Table 4.2 Advances and discounts to residents by sectors (million dinars)

End of year sectors	1979	1980	1981	1982	1983	1984	1985	1986	1987	1988	1989
Trade	523.5	671.8	843.2	955.3	948.8	987.7	932.8	920.2	962.1	967.2	975.4
Industry	91.3	159.2	174.3	193.6	148.2	144.9	122.2	106.4	140.3	136.1	135.2
Construction	332.2	408.0	523.2	763.4	664.2	683.2	680.0	701.1	784.7	813.7	743.7
Agriculture and fisheries	30.6	39.9	40.2	43.0	25.7	23.8	21.8	15.4	11.8	12.3	20.0
Financial and other services	120.9	142.8	236.0	269.9	314.1	360.6	360.9	371.4	465.5	362.0	347.4
Personal loans	520.1	620.7	890.3	1000.5	934.5	1040.4	1188.3	1254.0	1295.3	1346.7	1457.3
Real estate	254.3	306.6	371.2	614.5	683.4	742.8	768.6	816.5	838.5	912.4	902.6
Other	44.5	69.6	94.5	147.0	125.4	125.4	123.9	127.6	127.7	146.5	161.8
Total	1917.4	2418.6	3172.9	3987.2	3844.3	4108.8	4198.5	4312.6	4625.9	4696.9	4743.4

Source: Central Bank of Kuwait *The Kuwaiti Economy 1980–4.* Central Bank of Kuwait, *The Economic Report 1988.* Central Bank of Kuwait, Monthly/quarterly Review. 1990 figures not published due to Iraqi invasion.

53

KD 500 and KD 600 million by June 1984, these accounted for about 12 per cent of total domestic credit.

By June 1984, the Kuwaiti banks had also become net borrowers in the international markets, after allowing for syndicated lending and investments from foreign assets. The total net foreign currency cash and interbank assets minus syndicated loans and foreign investments had slipped to a negative figure of $US 183 million by December 1983 from a net surplus of $US 2.2 billion in June of the same year.

THE COMMERCIAL BANKS' RESPONSE

Loans to the 'Establishment'

Early in 1983, a credit facility of KD 150 million to the Establishment for Settlement of Forward Share Transactions was proposed. This facility was to provide a guarantee for the debts due to those referred to the Establishment from others who were not referred, but were illiquid. This facility was to be set up jointly by the banks for a period of one and a half years, which was the anticipated time it would take the Arbitration Committee to untangle the complex structure of inter-related debts.

As indicated earlier, the Establishment was founded by Decree 75 of 1983 to evaluate the assets of the referred debtors and to manage, reconcile and liquidate their assets and to settle with their creditors. The Establishment commenced issuing participation bonds and cash coupons, and the banks accepted these as collateral. However, in order to speed up final settlements the debtors of those referred also needed to be examined. The resulting facility created by the banks was to facilitate payments by such debtors also.

The facility took the form of a loan and was managed by the Industrial Bank of Kuwait as agent. It was disbursed by the banks to the Establishment in six tranches of KD 25 million each between October 1984 and January 1986. The Establishment was required to provide the Industrial Bank with a list of those debtors of a referred person who were granted a loan from the facility, but this list was not to be disclosed to the banks. The agent bank could, however, provide the bank with a list of those who subsequently abstained from settlement.

The Establishment was allowed to repay in full any tranche drawn down within two months without payment of any interest. Otherwise, interest at 10 per cent was payable effective from the drawn-down dates, and the Industrial Bank of Kuwait as agent could roll-over the facility for a further six months. If the borrower paid within six months, the banks were to accept payment and cancel the interest for the remaining period.

It was agreed that the KD 150 million facility was not a loan to the Establishment but more exactly a disbursement of funds through the Establishment. Moreover, by the middle of 1985, it became evident that numerous difficulties were being faced by the Establishment in getting many debtors of those referred to sign the required loan documentation or to introduce additional collateral. They would not even sign 'letters of admission of debts' before the notary public. The Establishment lacked the strict control system which would have been employed in a commercial bank, and had often disbursed loans prior to the completion of documentation. The banks took strong exception to this, but neither side could do anything to resolve the problem except to agree that the Establishment would follow up loans to ensure that documentation was completed early and would make no further disbursements to any debtor until after completion of the necessary documentation. In the meanwhile, the Central Bank exempted the KD 150 million loan from the law that no bank may extend credit facilities amounting to more than 10 per cent of its shareholders' funds, on a clean basis, to any one individual or institution.

In order to sort out the problems faced by the Establishment vis-à-vis debtors the banks contemplated seeking the aid of a notable law firm in Kuwait to follow up legal and other proceedings on collateral and loan collection. As at March 1986, the total draw-down on the facility by the Establishment was about KD 125 million, but total repayment was only KD 31 million (of which KD 30 million was principal, and KD 1 million was interest). The net amount outstanding was KD 95 million. The original number of borrowers was 240, out of which only 41 had repaid in full, and a majority had still not signed the documentation. The Establishment asked for a further period of three months until July 1986 to obtain more collateral and/

or to complete the documentation still outstanding.

By the third quarter of 1986 the role of the Industrial Bank of Kuwait as agent came to an end. Meanwhile, a further complication arose. By this time, some of the debtors of those referred had themselves been referred to the Establishment, or had come under the new Difficult Debt Settlement Programme (DDSP) announced by the Government (see later). As of April 1987, KD 86.3 million was outstanding on the loan, comprising: debtors qualifying under DDSP KD 37.7 million, debtors referred to the Establishment KD 27.1 million, and others KD 21.5 million.

If a debtor was referred to the Establishment and the required documentation was found to be incomplete, the file concerning that debtor was to be transferred to the Industrial Bank of Kuwait for their attention. In all other cases it was to be transferred to the bank having the maximum (or sole) exposure to that debtor.

Loans to KFTCIC and KIC

The commercial banks also granted a loan of KD 100 million each to the Kuwait Foreign Trading Contracting and Investment Company (KFTCIC) and the Kuwait Investment Company (KIC). This loan, disbursed in July 1983, was for a period of one year and was intended to help them in support operations after the Manakh débacle. It was later extended for a further year in 1984, and again in 1985 for a period of seven years, including a two-year grace period. This loan was also exempted from the 10 per cent maximum lending limit to any one person or institution mentioned earlier.

The discounting of Guarantee Fund bonds

As already discussed, the commercial banks started discounting the bonds issued by the Guarantee Fund for Forward Shares Transactions at 7.5 per cent, and either rediscounted them with the Central Bank at 7.25 per cent or carried them in their portfolio at face value.

The Guarantee Fund bonds so purchased by banks totalled

KD 500 million by June 1984 and reached KD 639 million by December 1985. In January 1984 KD 234 million worth of bonds had fallen due. These were renewed for two years by the Kuwait Investment Authority as agents for the Ministry of Finance. In addition, KD 203 million became due in January 1986, when it was decided by the banks to renew these bonds on a year-to-year basis, provided the Ministry of Finance would redeem them with the banks if the latter so desired.

Payments by the Kuwait Clearing Company

During late 1983, when the Clearing Company was arranging for the registration of cheques and claims, the banks suggested that the Company supply them with a list of the customers in the clearing system. This was agreed and the banks examined this list and identified their own customers who had been given credit facilities, with a view to obtaining part or full payment from disbursements made by the Kuwait Clearing Company to customers in surplus who were also bank debtors. In order to facilitate this all investors who were due to be paid by the Clearing Company had first to produce a Clearance Certificate from the banks. Through this procedure, the banks were able to make some recovery of debts in their classified portfolio.

Later, during 1984/5, the Government arranged for inspection in detail of the financial status, viability and operation of all closed shareholding companies in Kuwait with a view to reducing their numbers. It also offered to purchase, through the Clearing Company, shares of such closed companies at specified prices. The payment for these purchases was made either in cash or 50 per cent in cash and 50 per cent as shares in other companies.

Some investors were not willing to sell their holdings of closed company shares in this way as they considered the prices offered were too low. They preferred to cling on to them in the hope of higher prices later. Others wished to avoid paying the banks at any cost and were not willing to sell for cash, or cash plus shares, no matter what the price offered.

The banks and the Clearing Company also agreed a procedure by which the banks were provided with lists of those who sold shares. The banks then noted the names of those with debts exceeding KD 5,000 who were their debtors. The ownership of such shares was transferred to the Kuwait Investment Authority and 1 per cent of the value was deducted on sale and transferred to the Small Investors' Fund.

In the distribution of proceeds to the banks, priority was given to banks having a mortgage on any of the underlying shares. Any surplus left over, as well as the proceeds of unmortgaged closed company shares, was distributed to the banks, pro rata to the debts outstanding. This distribution was co-ordinated by the Central Bank at the request of the Kuwait banks themselves and the Kuwait Clearing Company.

Proposed investment holding company to purchase difficult debts

A proposal to establish an investment holding company to purchase difficult debts along with the associated collateral from banks and investment companies was made in May 1984. The purpose of the proposed company was to purchase the debts and associated collateral of banks' debtors who were illiquid, whether solvent or insolvent, as the banks were holding such debts in their books. Often, debtors could not service the interest on their loans, while the value of their mortgaged collateral was continuously falling.

The objectives of the proposed holding company were initially defined as:

1 Granting loans against acceptable collateral and purchasing shares from local banks' customers who lacked liquidity.
2 Purchasing shares from non-customers of banks who lacked liquidity to settle their positions with the Clearing Company, provided the ultimate beneficiary from such purchase would be a bank.
3 Guaranteeing to secure the banks' shares of referred bonds.

The capital and resources for this company were initially proposed at KD 600 million – KD 200 million each coming from the banks and the Government (KD 50 million equity and KD 150 million) and KD 200 million as rediscounting facilities with the Central Bank.

The advantages of establishing such a company were seen as follows:

1 Asset revaluation by banks could be carried out annually and not monthly.
2 Assets reflected as 'Other Assets' in a bank's balance sheet would, on transfer to the holding company, be shown under 'Loans and Advances', hence improving the balance sheet's structure.
3 Bulk shareholding would enable the holding company to influence for the better the operations of companies whose shares were held, and
4 Specialist attention would be available for this and related matters.
5 Such a move would overcome the Central Bank's restriction that such assets may only be held by the banks in their own names for a maximum period of three years.
6 Banks would be relieved from the pressure of those of its own shareholders who held such assets.
7 Bank managements would be freed to concentrate on commercial banking rather than spend time on what were, in effect, dead loans.

The disadvantages of the proposed company were seen as:

1 Banks could escape the consequences of poor credit judgement and dubious valuation.
2 Revaluation of assets prior to their transfer to the company could result in huge write-offs.
3 Difficulty in reaching unanimity in deciding which individual company's shares would be transferred. Shares in a particular company might be transferred to one bank but not another.
4 The biggest disadvantage of all, however, would have been the difficulty for banks to agree on the valuation of each other's assets. All banks would try to obtain the highest value for their own assets while arguing for a lower valuation of others.

There were also other important issues to be addressed:

1 How would the proposed company pay interest on the loans?
2 How would it apportion the proceeds of sales?
3 Who would decide whose assets to buy along with the debts?
4 How would the loans be eventually repaid?
5 How would the profits or losses on sale and valuation be apportioned?

The establishment of such a company was dependent on the solution of such complex problems. Hence the banks entrusted the task of conducting a feasibility study on the proposal to a reputed firm of chartered accountants in Kuwait.

A basic issue to be addressed, however, was the initial funding of the company. The Central Bank was not keen to participate in the funding, directly or indirectly, and maintained that the banks themselves should try to improve their assets, collateral coverage, etc. and utilise all their resources to reduce provisions and improve their profitability. Only as a last resort should they come to the Central Bank and the Government for support.

Hence, the banks re-worked the proposal with the main modification that the capital would be KD 100 million, with KD 50 million being paid up, to be subscribed by all the commercial banks and the three investment companies, pro rata to their domestic loan portfolios as at 31 December 1985.

It was proposed that the banks and investment companies offer the irregular debts (as per Central Bank classification) which they wished to sell on 30 June 1986. The company would purchase these at book value and issue discountable bonds for specific terms, Central Bank providing easy finance in proportion to the bonds owned by the institutions at a nominal rate not exceeding 1 per cent.

On maturity of each bond, the value would be settled between the holding company and the bank according to the loan market values at that time and in accordance with the criteria set by the company's board of directors. Any losses would be to the account of the bank or company while any profits would accrue to the company. Net profits would be distributed as 10 per cent to the shareholders and 90 per cent to the Central Bank.

After detailed discussions, this proposal was shelved in

favour of another proposal – for banks jointly to reschedule their difficult debts.

Framework of a plan for the joint settlement of difficult debts

The idea of arranging joint settlements by banks was first mooted in July 1985. The Bank of Kuwait and the Middle East and the Burgan Bank were entrusted with the task of preparing the preliminary draft of a scheme for joint settlement in cases where a bank's exposure was KD 3 million or more.

The first draft was ready by August 1985. It was drafted and re-drafted in various meetings of general managers of commercial banks constituting the Kuwaiti Banks Committee. Even by the end of 1985 the framework was not finalised. One basic issue was that the banks wanted debts above KD 2 million only to be covered, while the Central Bank wanted the limit to be as low as KD 500,000.

The meeting continued between the general managers, their chairmen and the Central Bank. Finally, the framework for a settlement of irregular joint debts was signed by the Chairman in January 1986. This was considered to be a protocol agreement between the banks as per the guideline (no instructions) of the Central Bank. The salient features of the agreement were as follows:

1 Joint settlement would be at the request of a debtor whose direct and indirect debts to the banks were not less than KD 20,000.
2 If a creditor bank owning 75 per cent of the debts of a debtor agreed to a settlement, it would be binding on the banks owning the remainder.
3 The bank with the maximum exposure would be the lead bank in each case. The lead bank would co-ordinate all meetings in evolving a settlement. This would be through a committee formed for each debtor from his creditor banks.
4 The Committee would work out the nature of the joint settlement based on the debtor's financial position, cash flows, etc. The debtor may be invited to attend meetings as necessary.
5 The maximum settlement period could be seven years, inclusive of a maximum grace period of two years.
6 Interest rate to be 7 per cent, with the possibility of a write-

off of interest in full or in part if a borrower was regular in payment and fully settled the debt, taking his final financial position into consideration.

7 The mortgaged collateral would continue to remain mortgaged to each respective bank, up to the limit agreed in the mortgage. Any surplus and any free assets would be charged to all banks pro rata to their exposure.

8 Guarantors would be required to participate in the settlement by guaranteeing the rescheduled debt.

9 If any legal suit existed against the borrower prior to joint settlement proceedings being initiated, the bank concerned could continue at its option with the legal proceedings.

The above framework of settlement did not cover customers having exposure to only one bank. The latter could adopt the framework to settle such outstandings at its own discretion.

The framework of settlement, though good in spirit, faced complex problems during its implementation. There was scope for different interpretations of many aspects of settlement and each bank adopted interpretations which suited its own interests. There were also problems created when a foreign creditor sued a debtor.

By May 1986, not a single joint settlement had been finalised. The banks were still splitting hairs on periods of settlement, loans, pricing free assets, voting percentages, etc. Even after the banks decided to concentrate on larger accounts with outstandings of KD 2 million or more, there was still no progress. Consequently, the Central Bank, directed by the Government, introduced the Difficult Debt Settlement Programme (DDSP).

THE CENTRAL BANK

Before discussing the Difficult Debt Settlement Programme, it would be relevant to touch upon some earlier measures taken by the Central Bank to strengthen and guide the development of the country's banking system. Many of these were introduced long before Al Manakh.

Maximum lending limit

As far back as 1976, the Central Bank had given the commercial banks guidelines on the maximum lending to be permitted to any one person or institution. This limit, covering unsecured facilities, was 10 per cent of a bank's own funds. Facilities guaranteed by the Government of Kuwait, foreign governments, first class foreign banks and Letters of Credit facilities were excluded from calculation of this limit. Also, the Central Bank had specified various percentage limits for various types of collateral, and such loans were to be subtracted from the total in each case to arrive at credit limits for the purpose of applying this directive.

Loans-to-overdraft ratio and credit quality

The Central Bank had also been concerned for some time about the mode of lending. With a view to ensuring that loans did not gravitate towards 'evergreen' overdrafts and that lendings were linked to repayments in instalments, the Central Bank specified that KD loans should be at least 45 per cent of total KD facilities by the end of 1980. This percentage was increased to 55 per cent in 1981 and 60 per cent in 1982.

The Central Bank also tried to establish both qualitative and quantitative controls over lending by, inter alia, requiring detailed statistics on the composition of domestic credit, and facilitating the formation of internal audit departments in the banks.

Loans against post-dated cheques

The Central Bank had, in May 1982, prohibited the banks from giving credit facilities against post-dated cheques and asked them to limit their banking functions as regards such cheques to payment or collection, for three reasons.

1 The cheque, according to Article 532 of Kuwait's Commercial Law, is an Instrument of Settlement, and therefore is due for payment at sight.
2 Allowing credit against post-dated cheques could create an impression among foreign banks that Kuwaiti banks discounted post-dated cheques or treated them as collateral.

This would adversely affect their confidence in Kuwaiti banks.

3 Such practices would increase the volume of credit for speculative and unproductive purposes, as previously illustrated.

Financing public issues of foreign companies and participating in closed companies

In May 1982, the Central Bank also directed the local banks to refrain from any action relating to public subscription in shares of foreign companies incorporated outside Kuwait, especially the granting of credit facilities to subscribers of such shares.

The Central Bank requested the banks to refrain from participating in the establishment of closed companies such as those set up during the last quarter of 1981 and which were trading in shares and real estate, directly or indirectly, on their own account.

Other measures

During 1980 and 1981, there was a great improvement in the banks' KD liquidity due to a marked growth in demand deposits. These grew by 122 per cent in 1981 and constituted a staggering 34 per cent of the total money supply (see Table 4.3) compared with a 20 per cent growth in 1979. This growth

Table 4.3 Annual changes in domestic liquidity and its components (%)

	1979	1980	1981	1982	1983	1984
Domestic liquidity	17.4	24.8	35.4	80	4.5	3.0
1 Money	4.6	6.9	81.4	−2.9	−5.6	−17.9
Currency in circulation	22.0	16.4	13.3	20.4	−0.6	−4.5
Demand deposits	−2.7	1.9	122.3	−10.0	−7.7	−23.8
2 Quasi-money	23.1	31.5	21.3	13.0	8.5	10.1
Saving deposits	−3.6	−9.8	12.9	9.5	20.6	−12.6
Time deposits	19.6	33.1	31.6	33.2	−3.5	11.5
Deposits in foreign currencies	96.2	65.3	1.2	−44.0	79.4	20.1
CD's in KD	−37.9	−20.2	53.8	25.2	5.2	12.4

Source: Central Bank of Kuwait, *The Kuwaiti Economy 1980–1984*.

in demand deposits coincided with the boom in the stock and real estate markets as well as with the rise in speculative deals and the possibilities of quick profits in these markets. In early 1982, these deposits reached an unprecedented KD 1,291 million.

Faced with the upward pressure on liquidity the Central Bank had decided in mid–1980 that local banks should maintain a specific minimum ratio (3 per cent) of all deposits forming part of the liquidity system as cash assets, i.e. cash, or balances with the Central Bank, or bills issued by the Central Bank.

The Central Bank also cut down the facilities it afforded to banks in the form of discounts, rediscounts and swaps, reducing these facilities from KD 500 million at the end of 1980 to KD 449 million in 1981 and KD 320 million in 1982. In contrast, local banks' claims on the Central Bank in the form of Central Bank bills and balances rose from KD 238 million in 1980 to KD 376 million in 1981 and KD 723 million in 1982 (see Table 4.4).

Table 4.4 Net financial position of local banks with the Central Bank (million dinars)

Particulars	1980	1981	1982	1983	1984
1 CBK claims on local banks	559.9	449.0	319.5	674.2	621.0
Discounts and rediscounts	298.6	282.4	276.7	334.6	359.0
(b) Swaps	301.3	166.6	42.8	339.6	74.0
(c) Money market transactions (deposits)	–	–	–	–	188.0
2 Local banks claims on CBK	237.5	375.8	732.2	476.2	467.9
(a) Balances with CBK	129.5	208.4	244.2	182.6	152.4
(b) CBK bills	108.0	167.4	488.0	293.6	246.8
(c) Deposits with CBK	–	–	–	–	68.7
3 Net balance[1] (2–1)		–362.4	73.2	412.7	–198.0 –153.2

[1] In the negative (−) means net KD injections by Central Bank into local banks.
Source: Central Bank of Kuwait, *The Kuwaiti Economy 1980–1984*.

Further, the Central Bank expanded its bills scheme in early 1982 by issuing a new type of seven-day bill in order to give the banks the opportunity of employing their surplus liquidity in short-term investments.

POST MANAKH

Fiscal and monetary measures

The post-Manakh years saw the imposition of a greater regulatory environment and a reassertion of Central Bank authority.

Due to the Al Manakh crash and the general economic recession world-wide, demand for domestic bank credit inevitably declined. This, plus the availability of liquidity, increased the demand for Central Bank bills. Accordingly, the local banks' holdings of such bills increased to a record KD 488 million by the end of 1982.

The Central Bank then tended to restrict cash facilities to local banks and swaps were reduced to 'Nil' during the first quarter of 1983, while discounts and rediscounts reached their lowest level of KD 239 million since the beginning of the last quarter of 1980.

The period from the second quarter of 1983 to the end of 1984 saw a continued decline in domestic economic activity and a deceleration in banking and financial activities. However, international interest rates and exchange rates – especially on the US dollar – tended to rise due to the contractionary policy of the US Federal Reserve and the demand for the dollar, both for investment and for repayments by debtor countries.

In Kuwait the KD deposit rates were kept at a low rate of 7.5 per cent by a 'gentlemen's agreement' between the banks with the tacit approval of the Central Bank, while the US dollar rates rose, resulting in an increase in deposits in foreign currencies, mainly the dollar, and in capital outflows. In 1983, deposits in foreign currencies with commercial banks increased by 79.4 per cent, as against a decline of 44 per cent in 1982. They further increased by 20 per cent in 1984 over 1983 (see Table 4.5). Conversely, KD deposits fell by 2 per cent in 1983 against an increase of 17 per cent in the previous year.

In order to counter these adverse movements, and to prevent abuse by commercial banks and exchange houses obtaining cheap dollars through Central Bank facilities, the Central Bank announced, in April 1984, a two tier dollar–dinar exchange rate.

A cheaper commercial rate of 0.295 dinar to the dollar was

Table 4.5 Some monetary indicators of commercial banks (million dinars; end of year figures)

Indicators	1980	1981	1982	1983	1984
Cash reserves in hand and with CBK	244.3	448.9	668.9	389.4	337.8
Claims on private sector	2671.4	3453.6	4292.5	4752.6	5045.4
(in KDs)	(2452.4)	(3098.1)	(3955.5)	(4451.0)	(4738.4)
(in foreign currencies)	(219.0)	(355.5)	(337.0)	(301.7)	(307.0)
Deposits of the private sector	2606.2	3583.0	3835.3	4027.1	4171.8
(in KDs)	(2018.3)	(2987.8)	(3502.3)	(3429.7)	(3454.0)
(in foreign currencies)	(587.9)	(595.2)	(333.0)	(597.4)	(717.8)
% of reserves to KD deposits	12.1	15.0	19.1	11.4	9.8
% of claims on private sector to deposits	102.5	96.4	111.9	118.0	120.9
% of KD claims on private sector to KD deposits	121.5	103.7	112.9	129.8	137.2
% of foreign currency claims on private sector to foreign currency deposits	37.3	59.7	101.2	50.5	42.8

Source: Central Bank of Kuwait, *The Kuwaiti Economy 1980–1984*.

offered to banks provided they could prove that dollars were needed for genuine commercial purposes, such as repayments under letters of credit. The other rate, the financial or free market rate, was as much as five points higher. Even for dollars obtained under this rate, the banks had to provide detailed information on the customer and the specific sums involved in dollar purchases.

The Central Bank also closed the swap facilities to banks that it considered to have abused the facilities and forbade the fifty or so exchange houses to deal on behalf of foreign financial institutions or foreign borrowers, and their access to cheap official dollars via the banks was effectively curbed.

The immediate result of these measures was chaos in the money market. The spread between bid and offer rates widened to as much as 4 per cent from the traditional ½ per cent. Dinar interest rates jumped from 7.5 per cent to as much as 12 per cent in order to counter uncertainties. Three months' inter-bank rates rose to an average of 10.7 per cent in June

1984, so that those whose credit facilities were rolled over in the middle of 1984 had to suffer the effects of higher pricing.

In order to ease the turmoil the Central Bank injected essential liquidity. Swaps and discounts soared to KD 685 million in the second quarter of 1984. The Central Bank also commenced giving loans to the commercial banks as required against a collateral of their holdings of Central Bank bills.

In August 1984, the two-tier rate was effectively scrapped, the Central Bank asserting that its measures were a success as they had protected the dinar against abusive speculation, had protected long-term investments abroad and had stemmed capital outflows.

The Central Bank had thus taken full advantage of the ammunition provided by the Manakh crisis to assert greater control over the banks and financial institutions, and had made effective use of the monetary and fiscal tools available to it. This strengthened confidence in the banking system as a whole, as subsequent developments were to show.

Loan classification and provisions

In 1985, the Central Bank had played a leader's role in co-ordinating and finalising the framework for joint settlement. But its major contribution in 1985 was in setting up precise and exact standards and definitions for classification in the credit portfolios of commercial banks and the calculation of provisions (and hence profits), the evaluation of financial investments and real estate portfolios, and the calculation of foreign exchange risks and provisions. Until then these calculations and evaluations were being undertaken by banks in their own individual way, subject of course to their being vetted by their external auditors and the Central Bank.

The Central Bank also laid down guidelines indicating when facilities should be considered irregular and when regular, when to take interest accrued to profits and when to keep it in a suspense account, when facilities should be considered secured and when unsecured, and how to make specific and general provisions, etc.

All the banks' year-end figures for 1985 were finalised according to these guidelines and vetted by the Central Bank. Only thereafter did the Bank allow the bonus/dividend distribution.

The directives of the Central Bank on loan classification and calculation of provisions were very conservative and strict, thus facilitating portrayal of a correct picture of a bank's financial position. The resulting figures of available provisions and reserves as against necessary provisions and reserves were not revealed but kept in confidence between the Central Bank and each bank. The banks were, however, urged to improve their profitability and to cut costs to the maximum.

The published accounts of most banks contained a note to the effect that:

> As at 31 December 1985, there was a shortfall between the provisions held for irregular debts and those required in accordance with instructions received from the Central Bank of Kuwait in December 1985 regarding classification of credit facilities and determination of provisions. The shortfall will be covered out of future years' earnings in accordance with the programme prepared by the Central Bank of Kuwait. As stated in the Difficult Credit Facilities Settlement programme, the Central Bank of Kuwait, on behalf of the Government of Kuwait, has undertaken to provide such support as may be required to secure the rights of depositors and to ensure that the shortfall does not ultimately result in a reduction in the level of shareholders' equity as disclosed by the banks' financial statements as at 31st December 1985.
>
> The financial statements have been prepared on this basis.

This, then, was the picture in 1985. In the few short years from 1982 the Central Bank, as the instrument of the Kuwaiti Government, had greatly extended its powers over the country's banking, and as a result of the Al Manakh débâcle had been forced to intervene on numerous occasions to maintain national and international confidence in the national banking system. Henceforth, it was destined to take an ever-increasing role in the management of national financial affairs.

DIFFICULT DEBT SETTLEMENT PROGRAMME

The most significant and important step in the ultimate and final solution of the Manakh débâcle was the Difficult Debt

Settlement Programme. This was announced by the Government to be effective on 10 August 1986.

The programme was applicable to all residents whose credit facilities with banks were irregular and whose financial positions were in deficit (i.e. their obligations exceeded their assets). It also applied to those whose debts may previously have been settled in accordance with the Central Bank's policies and the framework of joint settlement agreed upon by the banks in early 1986, provided the customer continued to be in deficit in his financial position at the time of settlement and such deficit continued until 10 August 1986. The programme did not cover consumer loans against salaries and wages, new facilities granted after 10 August 1986 and any increases in facilities approved after that date. Nor did it cover loans to borrowers whose financial position was in surplus after consolidation with the financial position of their guarantors, if any.

The format for the financial position statements was drafted by the Central Bank. The banks approached borrowers whose facilities were irregular, through registered letters indicating that they wished to settle their debts in accordance with the new programme. Each debtor was called upon to visit the bank which issued the letter to collect documents for a financial position declaration. The procedure for filling in their declaration statements was explained to them, as were the legal penalties should they provide inaccurate or misleading information, conceal the existence of assets or inflate the total value of their liabilities.

Each debtor was given two weeks to attend the appropriate bank to collect financial statement forms, and a further month to return them duly completed. The bank was allowed a further period of one month to prepare a final settlement programme based on the financial information and cash flow position of each debtor and to submit the programme to him. The debtor in turn was given two weeks in which to accept the settlement.

Each bank, when analysing the financial position of a debtor, was required to make a detailed analysis of all assets and liabilities indicated in the financial statement and the debtor's cash flow, to arrive at his surplus/deficit position. Only those with deficits were taken further into the settlement process.

Those with surpluses were considered not to qualify for the settlement programme and were dealt with as per credit accounts in the usual way, with irregularities to be regularised as soon as possible.

In the calculation of deficit or surplus for each debtor, the value of his residence acquired prior to debt was excluded; a private residence acquired after the debt was to be valued at a maximum of KD 400,000. For salary earners, not more than 25 per cent of their salary was to be deducted, provided the net salary left was not more than KD 1,000 per month. Lands and real estate were valued either by authorised valuation officers or in accordance with Ministry of Finance Resolution No.10 of 1986, at the time of settlement. Quoted securities were valued at market prices and unquoted securities at book values based on latest available financial statements.

In the event that there were other creditors of any particular debtor, the bank making the settlement was required to contact them with a view to representing them in the settlement. If any creditors initiated legal action against a debtor, the bank was to contact the Central Bank before initiating legal action itself.

The settlement was to be completed, authenticated and stamped in accordance with the Executive Formula. It was in two parts – the settlement loan for the value of the collateral as per Central Bank percentages, and an instrument of settlement called the Deferred Payment Instrument for the unsecured balance remaining.

A debtor was required to provide semi-annual, or at least annual, statements of his financial position once his settlement was finalised and the settlement loan raised.

His assets were to be revalued every year. The necessary amendments would then be made each year to the loan contract and the deferred payment instrument if the value of mortgaged assets rose or new cash flows materialised.

In a case of exposure to more than one local bank, the major creditor bank took the lead in the settlement process on behalf of the other banks, after obtaining details of each bank's exposure and associated collateral which remained mortgaged to them.

In joint settlements, the banks formed three committees to facilitate the process – the Joint Management Committee for high-level decisions, the Co-ordination Committee for the exchange of information on debtors and a Working Team Committee to prepare and analyse information and to propose settlements to the Joint Management Committee. The free assets were mortgaged to the order of the lead bank in favour of all participating banks, pro rata to their exposure, as was the debtor customer's free income such as rents.

The period of settlement and the interest chargeable were to be based on cash flow. In the case of debtors without regular cash flows the settlement loan was for ten years, interest free, up to the value of collateral assets. The deferred payment instrument was also to be for ten years, interest free. The former was repayable through liquidation of the assets before or at maturity of the loan (as per market conditions) or possession of the assets on maturity and any return from the assets thereafter. The latter was to be valued at the difference between the principal and the interest of debt due on settlement date and the value of all collateral assets. This instrument was to be written off at maturity or when a debtor had no funds to meet the outstanding balance.

As for debtors with regular cash flows the settlement loan was for fifteen years, up to the value of collateral assets, at an interest rate to be decided as per the debtor's cash flow, but not exceeding 7 per cent. The deferred payment instrument was also for fifteen years, interest free, and was equal to principal plus interest due on settlement date less the value of collateral assets. On maturity of the settlement loan this instrument was also to become due and to be written off or extended depending on the debtor's cash flow position at the time. In the event of appreciation in the value of collateral held, or a debtor obtaining increased cash flow, or a liquidation of assets, the debtor was to use the proceeds to meet partly or fully the deferred payment instrument, and thus reduce its value. If the debtor concealed any information on his cash flow, then the deferred payment instrument and the loan would bear interest at a rate to be approved by the Central Bank.

All settlement loans were vetted by the external auditors of each bank on behalf of the Central Bank, before being sent to the debtor for his assent. Debtors qualifying for this form of settlement were given until March 1987 to produce completed financial position statements. The banks were authorised to take legal action, after obtaining Central Bank's approval, against those debtors who did not give the required information within the specified time, or rejected the settlement offered, or gave inaccurate, misleading or incomplete information, or concealed information.

The Settlement Programme explicitly declared that the State was committed to maintaining the soundness of the Kuwaiti banks and their financial position, including the shareholders' funds, as declared on 31 December 1985, and guaranteeing the rights of bank depositors. The State indicated, through the Central Bank, that it would support each bank through various means. At the same time the Kuwaiti banks were required to build up, according to their abilities, provisions to cover the Deferred Payment Instruments and each year the Central Bank, acting on behalf of the Government, would be issuing net worth certificates to cover the difference between the total value of deferred payment instruments and the total of each bank's actual provisions, reserves and surpluses.

The Central Bank intensified its inspection of banks to ensure adherence to programme guidelines and to monitor its implementation. In the cases of joint settlements it had previously stipulated that if banks holding not less than 75 per cent of dues agreed to the settlement evolved by the lead bank, others had to agree. If such agreement was not reached, the matter was to be referred to a Supervision Committee for the Settlement Process set up by the Central Bank.

The Central Bank was to be the final authority for settlements involving board members and general managers of Kuwaiti banks.

OTHER MEASURES

In March 1987, the Central Bank reduced the lending rates to be charged by banks for KD facilities to residents as follows:

1 6 per cent for KD facilities up to one year, provided the facility was to be used for productive purposes.
2 7.5 per cent for KD facilities up to one year for all other loans.
3 1 per cent over KIBOR (Kuwaiti Interbank Offer Rate) for facilities over one year, whether for productive purposes or otherwise.

The above were maximum lending rates and could be less.

In addition, the maximum interest rates allowed for bonds, debentures and deposit certificates with maturity over one year were 2 per cent over KIBOR. Savings deposits were to be paid a minimum of 4.5 per cent. All Central Bank discounts and rediscounts were to be at 5.5 per cent. These directives were not applicable to facilities in foreign currency or facilities to non-residents.

The reasons for the lowering of interest rates were:

1 A general decline in KD deposit rates from an average of 9.3 per cent in December 1984 to 7.3 per cent in November 1986.
2 A general decline in dollar interest rates from an average of 10.1 per cent in December 1984 to 6 per cent in December 1986.
3 The need to reduce the interest burden on resident customers.
4 The need to revive private-sector demand for banking credit.

The Central Bank also stressed the importance of:

1 Strict adherence to the interest rate directives.
2 Granting credit facilities only after an accurate evaluation of a customer's position and business activities, and not resorting to 'name lending' as before.
3 Keeping unsecured facilities to any one person or institution within the maximum lending limit stipulated.
4 Establishing a formal and sound credit policy to reduce credit risks.
5 Establishing written investment policies with sufficient internal controls with a view to the maintenance of a desired level of liquidity at low risk.
6 Reducing staff and other expenses, except in areas which stimulate a bank's growth and increase its profitability.
7 Formulating an action plan to strengthen the banks' capital bases and to build up adequate provisions, improve the quality of assets and develop new areas contributing to profits.

After 1986, the Central Bank started to play an increasingly important role in controlling and guiding the banks (especially after the Governor, Mr Abdul Wahab Al Tammar, left and Sheik Salem Abdul Aziz Al Sabah took over as Governor) with a view to the softening and spreading over of the effects of the recession in general and the Al Manakh in particular. Its policy was to be 'soft but strict': 'soft' in that it would be providing full support through 'no interest' funds, swap and discount windows, etc., and 'strict' in the sense of ensuring implementation of its directives so that results would be forthcoming as the economy revived.

THE FOUR ACTORS IN THE DRAMA

As previous pages show, the drama of Al Manakh was spread over a number of years, with actors entering and leaving the stage as the various scenes unfolded. It would be enlightening to analyse the rationale behind the actions of four main groups involved and their long-term implications.

The investor

Has the investor learnt anything from the burning of his fingers in the Manakh? Is another Manakh a possibility after the market's fall in 1977 and its crash in 1982?

Some analysts discount the possibility of another Manakh because of the following:

1 The 'once-bitten twice-shy' attitude of the average investor.
2 Since the Manakh, the Government has acquired substantial share holdings in Stock Exchange listed companies. The banks also hold substantial holdings as collateral in view of the Difficult Debt Settlement Programme. Hence a run on share prices is effectively ruled out as 'floating stock' is limited, avoiding speculation.
3 The depression in real estate prices.
4 The ban on the use of post-dated cheques.

Others are of the opinion that in spite of the above factors, Manakh could still recur. They cite:

1 The inherent speculative nature of the investor in Kuwait who looks for speculative short-term appreciation of yields, rather than long-term growth.
2 Kuwait is expected to remain a capital surplus – low absorbent economy, with few domestic outlets for investments in manufacturing activity, and the prospect of investment in other spheres is expected to remain limited.

3 Above all, the local investor may feel psychologically secure in the knowledge that the Government bailed him out twice, so why not a third time?

The schools of thought both have their adherents and there is no firm consensus on who is right. It is only in the attitude and actions of the regulatory authorities, therefore, that the answer to the question 'can it happen again?' will be found.

The Government

Many observers feel that if the Government had enacted Law 100 of 1983 (reducing premiums on post-dated cheques to a maximum of 25 per cent) much earlier the Manakh problem would soon have been solved.

After the crash in August 1982, but prior to Law 100 of 1983, there were many debtors and creditors who had settled their accounts at premiums much higher than the 25 per cent level. The debtors who did so stood to lose, as they paid premiums higher than 25 per cent and hence were probably adversely affected in subsequent developments, such as becoming a debtor referred to the Establishment, or an illiquid creditor of a referred person, or could even end up as a debtor in the Difficult Debt Settlement Programme. Much of this would have been avoided if Law 100 of 1983 had been enacted sooner.

Another view is that the Government should have allowed the big dealers to go to the wall and allow events to take their own course. This would have resulted in more bankruptcies, but the country's economic and commercial affairs would have returned to their optimal levels much more quickly, relying more on normal market forces. Those who take this view consider that Government intervention has given rise to complacency among the Manakh players, who ought to have been allowed to feel the full force of market pressures.

The commercial banks

The banks certainly took full advantage of the oil boom years to make huge profits during the period 1975 to 1980. Hence there is a line of thought (to which the Central Bank, perhaps, subscribes) which holds that it is only equitable that the banks should bear the brunt of the Manakh crash and the recession. But the fact that the banks made huge profits during 1975–80 cannot justify their being made scapegoats in the post-Manakh era. In any case, once the Government had successively reduced the level of debts, first through the Clearing Company, then the Establishment and finally the Arbitration Committee and the law of 1983, it was inevitable and right that the banks should then attempt to spread the remaining effects over a ten- to fifteen-year period. However, Manakh or no Manakh, the banks to some extent can be held responsible for some of the bad or irregular debts. These cannot be fully explained away by the recession or the depression in oil prices. Prior to the Manakh crash all banks, faced with high liquidity, were scrambling to provide credit, and 'name lending' was rampant. Audited financial statements were hardly ever insisted upon by banks when making loans, even from established firms, lest they take their banking business elsewhere. Overdrafts tended to become evergreen, and loans were invariably made with 'bullet' repayment agreements, rather than repayment by instalments. Loans were also rolled over on a year-to-year basis. Exchange between banks of credit information on customers was sketchy and vague – phrases like 'good for normal business engagements' and 'very good reputation' were used for one and all.

It is now evident that the banks failed to work together to implement the Framework of Joint Settlement of Debts. In fact, they took an inordinately long time even to finalise the Framework! Hence it was inevitable that the Government and the Central Bank stepped in, and instead of seven-year loans at about 7 per cent interest proposed in the Framework, the banks ended up with ten- to fifteeen-year loans with zero or minimal interest earnings.

Central Bank of Kuwait

Although the Central Bank had formulated guidelines on the rationalisation of credit policy way back in 1977, it was not strict in their implementation. It had all the monetary tools of discounts, rediscounts and swaps available to it, as well as the power to decide liquidity norms for commercial banks, but it did not use them with any degree of effectiveness. It may be said, therefore, that it did not exert the full strength available to it to turn the direction of credit away from the speculation which lay at the root of the Manakh crisis. It was only when the speculative boom was at its peak that the Central Bank issued its directives on lending against post-dated cheques and Gulf shares. To that extent, therefore, the Central Bank could be considered indirectly culpable in not curbing the banks sooner.

Nevertheless, the Central Bank must be given credit in that, after the crash, it used the monetary tools at its disposal effectively, during times of both easy and tight liquidity. It was, unfortunately, caught between the high dollar rate abroad and the need for low KD rates domestically. A way out could have been to adopt exchange control measures, but short of that the next alternative was the two-tier exchange rate system which was adopted in 1984. Although this created chaos in the money market, it did achieve its aim of curbing cash outflows.

From 1985 onwards, the Central Bank had been tightening its control over commercial banks. Within a short time it had brought about uniformity in accounting, calculation of provisions, reporting, etc., and has since kept the banks on a tighter leash.

There was some justifiable resentment among banks that the Central Bank had almost taken over the commercial banks' role after the Difficult Debt Settlement Programme. It set the interest rates on deposits and advances, formulated the Difficult Debt Settlement Programme, vetted all bank policies on credit, investment, foreign exchange and even depreciation. Any legal action had to be referred to it before being implemented. By these measures the banks came more and more under the control of the Central Bank.

On the side of the Central Bank, it may be argued that it had no choice to act otherwise as the banks were not acting in co-ordination with each other in their approach to any issue, nor did they act fast enough.

On the whole, it appears that Central Bank control has brought some cohesion and uniformity to the commercial banking system, but this could not subsist in the long run. After the Difficult Debt Settlement Programme there was a big mismatch in the asset and liability structure of the banks. The assets are mainly longer term, three to five years or more,

78

while the liabilities are mainly deposits of one year or less. The Central Bank has to address this problem. It was also expected to issue broad guidelines each year on the sectional distribution of credit and to be specific about the help it could render to the banks, and to introduce its policies well in advance so as to avoid disruptions caused by abrupt introduction of measures such as the two-tier exchange rate system mentioned earlier. These measures would greatly assist the development of the commercial banking system and would be further enhanced by the Central Bank and the commercial banks if they not only arranged regular meeting at Governor/Chairman or Governor/General Manager levels, but did so at operational levels also. For example, at Operations/Treasurers or Heads of Banking Operations/Assistant General Managers levels to ensure a mutually beneficial exchange of views in specific areas.

CONCLUSION

In the preceding pages we have touched upon the phenomenal growth of Kuwait's Capital Market which led to the dizzy heights of Al Manakh, the subsequent crash and the measures taken by the banks and the Central Bank to mitigate its after-effects. These measures had to be introduced in conjunction with others to counteract the effects of a world-wide recession which set in while the whole Kuwaiti economy was reeling from the blow already dealt by the Al Manakh crisis. But, whatever the shortcomings of Al Manakh, and no matter how wise pundits may now be as to what ought to have been done, there is no doubt that the crisis has had two important results:

1 It led to very close cooperation between the Government, the banks and the Central Bank, co-operation that has stood the country in good stead when facing the economic recession which closely followed it.
2 Coming at the end of the oil boom years, it led Kuwaitis to a more rational approach to Government expenditure and public spending, thus emphasising the high degree of economic and political stability of the country.

It also taught a sharp lesson to the Kuwaiti investor, i.e. there is nothing wrong with speculation, but only to the extent that such speculation is backed by available resources. As the saying goes in Arabic, 'only stretch your legs as long as the blanket'.

Sadly, all efforts by the Government, the banks and the Central Bank are past history. All efforts to counter the effects of Al Manakh and the world recession were brought to nought on a fateful day in August 1990 by one man, Saddam Hussein, through the invasion of Kuwait. The effects of Al Manakh and the recession pale into insignificance compared with the effects of the invasion, to which we turn later, but before doing so it may be worthwhile reminding ourselves of the uncanny similarity of Al Manakh with the South Sea Bubble calamity which hit the London stock market in 1720.

THE SOUTH SEA BUBBLE

In the second half of the seventeenth century, Britain had seen an unprecedented avalanche of new patents being granted, some of which formed the basis of the Industrial Revolution which was to follow some hundred years later. At the same time, the concept of the Joint Stock Company was being fostered, and also new concepts in the creation of credit. Borrowing for investment became very profitable, and as more and more companies were established for the development of newly patented inventions, so did the 'inventions' become more obscure, so that by the early part of the eighteenth century the practice of floating companies to take advantage of credit available, rather than for purposes of genuine productive investment, had become well established. A company had previously been formed in the City of London to foster and conduct trade with South America. This was 'The South Seas Company'. War had reduced its activities to a minimum, and its handlers sought new avenues for their talents. They hit upon a scheme for converting the National Debt into company stock by a purchase from the Government, but in fact they did not actually have the money available. Instead, they intended to borrow it. This they did, and while the whole saga would fill several volumes, suffice it to say that in order to pay off the initial borrowing further loans were raised to pay both principal and interest. Worse, paper issued by the company was used as collateral for further loans, so that the process became never-ending. Speculation fever gripped the market

80

and monies flowed in from other markets in Europe. New companies were formed with increasingly bizzare intentions, one even claiming to be for a purpose so profitable it would not be disclosed until all subscriptions had been received!

The inevitable crash came, as in Kuwait, when a debt was presented for payment on maturity and it could not be honoured. A run on the banks commenced and those who had lent on the collateral of the falling stocks were unable to transfer them into liquid funds. Over half of London's banks closed their doors and the repercussions were felt throughout Europe. Great families in Britain found themselves ruined and many prominent members of the Government were disgraced. But, again as in Kuwait, the task of extricating the market from the chaos which it had brought upon itself fell on the Bank of England with the assistance of some of the more stable national institutions. The Government did not take a leading role, but lent its assistance when required.

It was on the experience gained during this period that the Bank of England established the reputation which assisted in later establishing London as the world's foremost financial centre for some two hundred years, and with the legislation it fostered and the practices it developed it set the pattern for national control of banking and commerce throughout the world. Kuwait has gone through a similar experience. The lessons learnt, if translated into action, may result in establishing a base for national financial development on a long-term basis, replacing the short-term speculative approach which had bedevilled the financial sector in the past.

5

THE IRAQI INVASION AND ITS AFTERMATH

Although this book's main emphasis is on the economic and financial aspects of the crises which have hit Kuwait since 1980, the author would be failing in his duty if he did not cover in some detail the barbaric invasion of Kuwait on 2 August 1990, the terror and looting during the months of occupation which followed, the developments in the international arena during that period and the final rout of the invader.

The war has caused a total rethink of Kuwait's future development, so that after detailing the devastation of Kuwait – physical, environmental and psychological – some account of the process of reconstrucion and rebuilding now being undertaken, in the light of Kuwait's revised programme for the future, will be given.

PRE-AUGUST 1990

Kuwait had always been a very staunch supporter of Iraq during the Iran–Iraq war. Moreover, Kuwait had also helped Iraq with a large number of soft loans, both on a Government-to-Government basis and on commercial terms through Kuwaiti commercial banks.

Even in those days, Iraq had been an international 'pariah' or outcast, and very few western commercial banks were willing to lend to the country, as repayments were not forthcoming due to its continuing foreign exchange crises and resultant controls. Iraq was again and again rescheduling its debt, basically because on one hand its economy was in ruins due to the war with Iran, and on the other oil prices were depressed.

Kuwait had also helped Iraq indirectly by absorbing Iraqis into various sectors of its economy. It appeared to be a perfect example of Islamic brotherhood. The President of Iraq, Saddam Hussein, and HH the Amir of Kuwait were often seen in various Arab and international forums, shaking hands and posing together for photographs.

So the question arises, 'Why did Saddam invade Kuwait?' The full answer may never be known but several reasons may be offered, all or any of which may be appropriate:

1 The Iraqi army, numbering one million after the cessation of the Iraq–Iran war, was unoccupied and was getting restless. It could perhaps overthrow Saddam. Hence, a 'prize plum was offered for the picking' in the neighbourhood.
2 Iraq had been claiming that Kuwait was 'stealing' its oil income by exploiting the Rumaila oilfields, which are on the Kuwait–Iraq border.
3 It filed a claim with the Arab League alleging that Kuwait had stolen $2.5 billion in Iraqi crude from Rumaila by exploiting the circumstances of the Iran–Iraq war.
4 Iraq wished Kuwait to write off debts totalling $21 billion. This Kuwait was unwilling to do. In fact in May 1990 Kuwait asked Iraq for repayment.
5 Iraq had constantly claimed that Kuwait historically was always a part of Iraq, and when not claiming the whole of Kuwait it was disputing the delineation of Iraq–Kuwait borders, especially after the cessation of the Protectorate Agreement with Britain in 1961.
6 Most importantly, Saddam wished to prove that he was the 'de facto' King of the Arab world, a status last attained by Gamel Abdul Nasser of Egypt.

During the early part of 1990, Iraq and Kuwait had several brotherly meetings to sort out the differences relating to border demarcation, the share of oil in the Rumaila oilfield and the Kuwaiti loans to Iraq. At no time up to August 1990 was there any indication that Iraq would take the extreme but foolish step of invading its peaceful neighbour. The last of these meetings was in Jeddah at the end of July 1990. The Iraqi representative walked out of the meetings, saying 'you will see more of us soon' – and at midnight between 1 and 2 August 1990, the invasion of Kuwait began.

THE INVASION AND OCCUPATION

In the early hours of 2 August 1990 Iraqi forces stormed into Kuwait with over 150,000 troops, hundreds of tanks, guns and aircraft.

The invasion began with the capture of Kuwaiti border posts along the state's northern and western borders with Iraq. The Iraqi air force straffed the runways at the Kuwaiti international airport. Other targets were the communications building at Sabahiya, the Crown Prince's palace on Arabian Gulf Street, etc. By dawn of 2 August 1990 the Iraqi troops had entered the city and taken over key points such as hospitals, the headquarters of the Public Authority of Ports, the Information Ministry Complex, the Sief Palace and the Ministries of Interior and Foreign Affairs.

Some of the members of the ruling family, including HH the Amir, HH the Crown Prince and the Prime Minister, were able to escape to neighbouring Saudi Arabia. The armed forces of Kuwait, numbering around 15,000, stood no chance as they were hopelessly outnumbered.

By 4 August 1990 Kuwait was cut off from the outside world as the Iraqis destroyed the Umm Al Aish earth satellite station, although communications within Kuwait were maintained throughout the occupation. However, members of the Royal Family and other prominent citizens within Kuwait were able to maintain contact with the outside world, at great risk to themselves, through secret satellite phones and a ham radio network.

THE EARLY MONTHS

The early days were pandemonium. The Iraqi troops, led by the Republican Guards, looted the Gold Souk on the first night, while their supporters danced in the streets. People acted on instinct and rumours spread like wild fire. Artillery and automatic weapon fire broke out spontaneously and Iraqi troops bulldozed buildings suspected of harbouring resistance snipers.

A clandestine radio repeatedly called for international help before being knocked off the air. A boy died in a suicide attack by ramming his car into an Iraqi truck, killing 20 Iraqi soldiers. Store shelves were stripped as Iraqi soldiers looted supermarkets and sold goods on the streets outside. A shortage of foodstuffs was feared, but entrepreneurial Iraqis and Jordanians brought fruits, bread, etc. to sell in Kuwait at enormous profits. 'Iraqi hunting' became a night-time craze, with Kuwaiti teenagers indulging in 'hit and run' raids. A number of Iraqis were captured and held in the basements of houses. Some, who defected, were later released with false papers and civilian clothes, others were executed. One Iraqi soldier was killed with a Beduin sword as he ate dinner at a backstreet restaurant.

Most of the Iraqi soldiers, except the Republican Guards, were merely famished teenagers carrying rifles. They were so poorly treated that they would bang on doors and beg for food, and so poorly trained that their favourite pastime was to throw photographs of HH the Amir of Kuwait in the air and try to shoot them, or to consider themselves as Clint Eastwood or Lee Van Cleef and shoot Coca-Cola tins tossed skywards in the same fashion.

Escape was on everyone's mind. At one point, cars from Kuwait were four abreast, 30 kilometres deep, at the Saudi border, moving only 20 kilometres in three hours. Initially, the embassies had no evacuation plans, so people had to make their own. Some got out with the help of Beduin guides, others paid middlemen money to arrange their crossing or even bribe Iraqi soldiers who had set up a sideline, but not everyone who tried made it. One couple lost their children due to exposure in the desert, before they themselves were rescued by helicopter. Another Pakistani couple were pushed over the border by Iraqi guards, who held back and continually raped their two daughters for two days before sending them back into the city.

Slowly, each community began to organise itself, improvising as the social and administrative infrastructure had crumbled. Night patrols were set up to guard against looters who roamed the city. These would bring empty trucks or trailers and break open and plunder unoccupied residential houses and shops. They would load the trucks at night and in the morning they would drive away with impunity.

Everyone dreaded the 'midnight' knock by an Iraqi. Such a knock usually resulted in looting the home, raping the females and killing the males. Those that were lucky got away with just a demand for food. Car owners were asked to hand over their keys at gunpoint. Thousands of cars were stolen from residents and showrooms. Several motor distributing premises and showrooms were set ablaze. Some car dealerships let it be known through the grapevine that they would supply four-wheel drive vehicles to Kuwaitis on a signature and a promise to pay after the crisis. This was considered better than losing them to the Iraqis, who had already driven away with the other models.

Kuwaitis themselves organised district groups to offer services. Some semblance of medical care was organised for the public although Iraqis had carted away most of the medicines and equipment. Co-operative Societies organised food supplies and began rationing. Money was collected for those in need and for the first time boys collected trash for burning.

Organised resistance movements evolved on a district basis but were never part of a central command. Most were led by former police officers and army men with weapons training, but the resistance met with a brutal campaign of retaliation. When the bodies of four Iraqi soldiers were found in a school, four houses directly across the street were destroyed.

When one of two Iraqi women who had provided hot food to Iraqi troops was killed, a father and his three sons who lived near the field where her body was found were shot. Prominent resistance leaders were killed and bodies hung in public places such as Safat Square. Anyone suspected of working with the resistance was killed, along with selected family members. Others were left to tell the tale.

Many Kuwaitis died with a single bullet in the head but physical and mental torture were the order of the day. 'I saw the sun at night and stars in daytime,' said one Kuwaiti with a long scar cut across his forehead by a gunshot. His crime was his close association with the Government in exile. Another teenage boy was found with a picture of the Amir. He was held for three days and then brought home by the Iraqis. As he ran up to greet his mother, he was shot in the back and died in her arms.

On 2 September 1990, the resistance planned a show of defiance. Kuwaitis and other Arab nationals were asked to climb to the roofs of their villas and apartment buildings at midnight. Together, they would cry out to God with a call that has echoed down the centuries from martyrs of Islam on the hundreds of battlefields that have tested their faith.

'Allah – O – Akbar', God is Great

Word of this passed through whispers in co-operatives, mosques and diwaniyas. Even the BBC announced plans for the protest. Just before midnight it all began. A sweep of a torch beam from a roof top and a lone voice calling 'Allah O Akbar' shredding the night silence to be followed by a deafening crescendo of voices, 'Allah O Akbar' again and again, for one full hour. Some say Kuwait was born anew that night.

EFFORTS TO DESTROY THE IDENTITY OF KUWAIT

From the first day of the invasion the Iraqi regime issued a series of resolutions aimed at eradicating the very name of Kuwait itself. On 2 August an announcement was made that the Kuwaiti Government had fallen as a result of an internal revolution in Kuwait. Iraqi soldiers were telling the Kuwaiti people 'we came to save you and support the popular revolution'. The Iraqi dictator then invited certain Kuwaiti individuals who had opposed the June 1990 National Council elections, and who had attended the Baghdad celebrations to mark the July anniversary of the Ba'athist revolution, to form a Government. But these individuals, while admitting certain differences with their Government, emphasised that such differences were to be solved within the family of Kuwait and needed no outside intervention. They refused to align themselves with the Iraqi dictator.

So the Iraqi regime installed what it called the 'Provisional Free Kuwait Government'. The next step was to announce that once this Government was installed, Iraqi troops would leave Kuwait from 5 August 1990. Revolutionary Command Council issued a resolution 'annexing' Kuwait to Iraq and designating it 'the 19th governorate' and renaming Kuwait City as Kazimah, claiming that Kuwait had always been a part of Iraq.

Saddam's claim was a betrayal which had no equal in history. (On 4 October 1963, Iraq had recognised Kuwait as a free independent sovereign state and signed an agreement to this effect, which was filed with the United Nations.) Saddam's cousin, Ali Hassan Al Majeed, was appointed military governor of Kuwait. He was the man responsible for the unprecedented genocide of Kurds during the 1988 Kurdish uprising.

In the meanwhile, in the Arab League summit held on 10 August 1990, no firm resolution to call for the Iraqi withdrawal could be agreed. But this was a blessing in disguise for Kuwait, as it came to know who its true friends were in the Arab world. Two days later Baghdad radio made an announcement linking any withdrawal to a solution of the Palestinian problem. Furthermore, Saddam sought to make peace with Iran by withdrawing thirty brigades of his army from the Iraq–Iran borders on 17 August 1990 to supplement his occupation forces in Kuwait. But Iran was wary of this newly expressed cameraderie of its former enemy and maintained a neutral stand throughout the Gulf crisis.

As part of their efforts to obliterate Kuwait's identity, Iraq issued various orders:

1 All military personnel from the Ministries of Interior and Defence – except the National Guard – were ordered to return to work.
2 Kuwaitis were asked to surrender their weapons: those who did not do so were liable to execution.
3 The appointments of civil servants not reporting for duty were to be terminated.
4 Any house from which shots were fired was liable to be destroyed along with surrounding properties.
5 Kuwaitis were ordered to take their cars to the traffic department to be issued with new Iraqi number plates and registration papers. Garages were barred from attending to cars with Kuwaiti number plates and petrol stations were barred from filling them.

The repression of Kuwaitis was very severe. It included:

1 Eviction of hospital patients to make room for Iraqi casualties. Strict control over admissions in hospitals to detect any resistance fighters attending for treatment.
2 Indiscriminate robbing of cars at gunpoint.
3 House searches at random to lower the morale and break the back of the resistance. Anyone found with a photocopier

was liable to execution as photocopiers could be used to print resistance newsletters.

4 Capture and torture of Kuwaitis and execution of suspected resistance fighters, and the hanging of their bodies in public squares.

At the end of September 1990 the Revolutionary Command Council ruled that the Kuwaiti dinar was no longer legal tender and would be withdrawn from circulation from 6 October 1990. The Kuwaiti dinar could be exchanged for the Iraqi dinar on a one to one basis. The excuse given for this was that Kuwait's Government had forced down the value of the Iraqi dinar to 1/25th of the KD value. This was of course untrue. The Iraqi dinar had steadily fallen in value due to Saddam's wars, his military adventures and his mismanagement of the Iraqi economy.

As part of its efforts to 'Iraqise' Kuwait, the new governorate of Kuwait was segmented into three districts, Kazimah (Kuwait City), Jahra, and Al Nidaa. A number of deputies were attached to each district. Many residential suburbs, streets, schools and hospitals had their names changed. The suburbs were called quarters as in Iraq and their names changed as follows:

Salmiya	Al Nasr Quarter
Sabah Al Salem	Al Thawra Quarter
Khaldiya	Al Jumhouriya Quarter
Shuwaikh	Al Rasheed Quarter
Salwa	Al Khansa Quarter
Jabria	Ahrar Quarter
Ahmadi Township	Al Nida Township

Salem Al Mubarak Street became 17 July Street. Faisal Bin Abdul Aziz Street became Babil Street, Hamad Al Mubarak Street became Saqr Quraisn Street, and so on. Shuwaikh Port became Al Rashid Port, the Mubarak Al Kabir Hospital became Al Fidaa Hospital and the Sabah Hospital became Saddam Hospital.

Kuwaitis were given a deadline of 23 November 1990 to exchange their Kuwaiti identity documents for Iraqi papers showing their Iraqi nationality. Those who did not do so were punished severely. Expatriates were asked to report to an 'Arab

90

Affairs Section' to exchange their residence permits for Iraqi documents.

Saddam stated that Kuwait was part of Iraq and had no separate identity as a nation. Hence all foreign embassies in Kuwait were ordered to be closed within four days from 20 August 1990. Western embassies that refused to oblige were put under siege and their water supply and electricity cut off. Later, as the world's consternation grew, Iraq began rounding up and transporting westerners to hold as hostages. These were taken to strategic locations in Iraq and Kuwait such as petrochemical complexes, telecommunication centres, military installations and oil installations.

Besides looting individual houses the Iraqis turned their attention to Kuwait's treasures and public property. The Kuwait Institute for Scientific Research was completely looted and emptied of its renowned research equipment and library. The Kuwaiti National Museum was denuded of its jewellery, pottery, seals, books, manuscripts and paintings. Sculptures dating back to 300 years BC were vandalised.

The priceless Al Sabah Collection, the most comprehensive collection of Islamic arts in the world, was looted and removed. Iraqis set fire to two of the four main buildings in the museum complex. The cost of the damage is estimated to be over KD 1 billion, while the treasures themselves are priceless and irreplaceable.

The recordings and library tapes from Kuwait Radio and Television were looted. Nearly all the equipment was stolen. Kuwait gold bullion valued at over KD 950 million was carted away. Over KD 350 million in KD bank notes was reportedly removed to Iraq. The fleet of over 2,500 buses of the Kuwait Public Transport Company was driven away to Iraq.

Kuwait Airways commercial aircraft were also flown to Baghdad. The airport's navigation and control systems were wrecked. Kuwait University was plundered, its books, equipment, even furniture taken away. The animals in Kuwait zoo were either eaten or starved to death. Private shops and shopping malls were looted and set on fire. Special attention was given to gold shops and car, furniture and electronic showrooms. Spare parts, equipment and instruments were taken away from Kuwait's oil refineries. Alcohol, which is banned in

Kuwait, was made freely available and soliciting and pimping of prostitutes also began.

The Secret Police started surveillance of worshippers at Friday prayers and forced preachers to praise Saddam for his holy war, or Jihad. Kuwaitis often had to pay ransom money amounting to thousands of dinars to free their chilren from Iraqi kidnappers. The Iraqi regime published the *Al Nidaa* newspaper to foster the speeches of Saddam Hussein and to act as a mouthpiece for the Ba'ath Party. This newspaper was printed on the *Al Qabas* newspaper printing presses and distributed free. Propaganda speeches and songs were broadcast through three radio stations. The Voice of 'Al Madina Al Munawara' was aimed at Saudi Arabia, while the 'Voice of Peace', in English, was aimed at the local non-Arab expatriates and the coalition forces. A third programme was broadcast by the Mother of Battles Station, which commenced broadcasting as soon as the war began.

As it became known that Iraq had no intention of leaving Kuwait, the expatriates were left with no jobs, no salaries, no schools and little food. The exodus of expatriates from Kuwait and Iraq then began. Due to economic sanctions imposed by the United Nations, no flights were operating out of Iraq and Kuwait. Communication lines with the rest of the world were also cut. Thousands of expatriates fled Kuwait and Iraq by bus or car or any other means of transport available. Most reached Amman, which is about 1,500 kilometres from Kuwait. Thousands suffered in makeshift refugee camps in Jordan before they could board planes to their home countries. Accounts of the human misery at the camps – lack of water and sanitation, lack of food and exposure to the merciless sun – could no doubt fill volumes. It was one of the largest evacuations of people in history.

6

THE WORLD RESPONSE

The entire world, with the exception of a few countries such as Yemen, Cuba, Djibouti, Sudan and Jordan, condemned the invasion and annexation. The Security Council of the United Nations passed its Resolution 660 directing Iraq to make an immediate and unconditional withdrawal from Kuwait. The initial response of Iraq was to declare Kuwait to be an integral part of Iraq and its nineteenth province. But as world pressure mounted Iraq began linking its occupation to the Palestinian question, asking why the United Nations adopted double standards – imposing sanctions on Iraq, while allowing Israel to continue to be in the occupied lands of Palestine despite the United Nations resolutions to the contrary.

The stalemate continued as the United Nations imposed more economic sanctions. Resolution 662 declared the annexation of Kuwait null and void, Iraqi assets were frozen the world over and many countries severed or greatly reduced their diplomatic links. Ships of the western nations, led by the USA, began to police the Gulf waters, while a large contingent of American air force planes began surveillance of the airspace around Iraq to stop any aircraft violating sanctions by carrying goods into the country.

The USA and its western allies then started massing their troops in Turkey and Saudi Arabia. The landing of troops in Saudi Arabia was at the invitation of the Saudi Government, as it feared that the Iraqi juggernaut would roll into Saudi Arabia after overwhelming Kuwait. The operation was known as 'Desert Shield', and in the event the Iraqi invasion of Saudi Arabia did not happen.

During the five months after the Iraqi occupation the United

93

Nations passed as many as twelve resolutions, significant among which was the right of members to use all possible means to secure Iraqi withdrawal (Resolution Number 678).

In the meanwhile peace efforts continued, with France assuring that it would take up the Palestinian issue once Iraq withdrew. The Soviets also came up with the following significant proposals:

1 Iraq unconditionally to withdraw from Kuwait.
2 The Soviets would raise the Palestinian question in future world forums including the United Nations.
3 The guarantee of Iraq's borders.
4 There would be no guarantee for Saddam Hussein, but he would not be tried for war crimes. In effect, that would mean the Iraqi regime would be maintained.

In response, the Revolutionary Command Council stated that Iraq had decided to accept Security Council Resolution 660 of 1990, including the clause relating to Iraqi withdrawal, provided:

1 Allied forces withdrew from Saudi Arabia.
2 Syrian troops withdrew from Lebanon.
3 Israel withdrew from occupied Palestinian lands.

President Bush dismissed this Iraqi response as a 'serious hoax', having not only unacceptable 'old conditions' but new conditions as well. He refused to recognise the linkage of Iraqi withdrawal with other problems. He indicated that until a massive visible withdrawal by Iraq was made allied forces, under United Nations Resolution 678, would continue their efforts to force Iraq's compliance. He also asked the Iraqi people to take matters into their own hands and force Saddam Hussein to step aside. Effectively President Bush was advocating a military coup in Iraq. He also proceeded to obtain the sanction of the US Congress for effecting a full-scale ground offensive. In the meanwhile, the US troop concentration in Saudi Arabia reached 360,000 and allied troops from twenty-eight nations reached 100,000, all backed by heavy artillery, tanks and air power. The naval might of the USA and the west stood off the coast of Kuwait.

On 29 November 1990 the United Nations passed a historic Resolution authorising the use of 'all necessary means' to secure the liberation of Kuwait, and set 15 January 1991 as the deadline for the Iraqi withdrawal. Diplomatic efforts to avert a war continued, President Mitterand of France proposed an Iraqi withdrawal under United Nations supervision. It was proposed that the US Secretary of State, Mr James Baker, meet Mr Saddam Hussein or Mr Tariq Aziz, Foreign Minister of Iraq, on a date to be chosen by Iraq, while the USA would pick a date for Mr Tariq Aziz to come to the USA. The USA gave fifteen dates, but none were acceptable to Iraq, which insisted that Mr Tariq Aziz could come only on 12 January. This date, being too close to the United Nations deadline, was unacceptable to the USA. Finally, the meeting did take place in Geneva on 9 January 1991, as a last step to find a political solution to the crisis. After the meeting Mr James Baker, the US Secretary of State, told the waiting world he had 'come to communicate with Iraq, not to negotiate. The message had been conveyed to Iraq that it had to withdraw peacefully or be expelled forcibly.' Regrettably there was nothing to suggest Iraqi flexibility on complying and Mr Baker added that 'Iraq had

1 Miscalculated the international response to the invasion, and expected the world to stand idly by.
2 Miscalculated the response to the barbaric policy of holding foreigners as hostages.
3 Miscalculated in its hope that it would divide the international community.'

Mr Baker ended by saying that 'the choice is now with Iraq – to risk military confrontation or to leave Kuwait.'

Mr Tariq Aziz, Foreign Minister of Iraq, spoke to the press after Mr James Baker. He stated that Iraq did not miscalculate; it knew everything; one can only talk of bringing peace to the region by talking of all problems, such as the Palestinian question covered by United Nations Resolution 242 of 1967 and 368 of 1973, which had not been implemented. The USA did not take any measures against Israel. It concentrated only on what Iraq was supposedly holding – chemical, biological or nuclear weapons – but not on what Israel had. He ended by saying that the USA followed double standards and Iraq would not yield to threats.

Mr Tariq Aziz did not touch upon Iraq's looting of Kuwait or on its withdrawal. He did however add that he had refused to accept from Mr Baker the letter which he had brought from President Bush to President Saddam Hussein as 'the language of the letter did not conform to the language normally used between Heads of States; politeness does not contradict substance.'

THE AIR WAR

The air war of 'Operation Desert Storm' began on 16 January 1991. It was a grossly one-sided affair, with the allied air forces having complete control of the skies within a matter of days.

Thousands of sorties were flown to bomb strategic locations in Iraq and Kuwait; among the places bombed were military installations, bridges, telecommunication centres. Regrettably, some civilian areas were also bombed, in the belief that they concealed military installations. For example, a public shelter was bombed, its fifteen feet thick concrete ceiling penetrated, killing hundreds of civilians taking shelter there. Iraq gave maximum exposure in the media to the bombing of shelters, a milk factory, etc., and Jordanian support for Iraq intensified after the air war began.

Iraq's response to the air war was muted. Iraqi anti-aircraft fire claimed a few allied bombers, especially the low flying British Tornados. But its most significant act was the launch of Scud missiles by mobile Scud launchers on Israel and Saudi Arabia. Over forty missiles were fired on these two countries. This was a deliberate ploy to involve Israel in the crisis and thereby create a split in the allied coalition which included anti-Israel nations such as Syria. But Israel was held in check by the USA and did not retaliate.

The Scud missiles themselves did little damage, except one which landed in a military camp in Saudi Arabia. Most Scuds were detroyed by the US Patriot missiles before they could cause any damage. The Patriots were seventeen feet long surface-to-air missiles with a 200lb payload. The Scuds were picked up by US surveillance radar and then tracked by Patriot radar command. Within minutes the Patriots would be launched and the interception completed.

The allied coalition intensified the air war by flying over 300 sorties per day. No Iraqi plane had made any ground attack on allied forces. Iraqi artillery, armoured carriers, etc. became 'sitting ducks' in face of the allied pounding. Over half of the bridges across the Euphrates river in Baghdad were destroyed. Baghdad became a city under seige, with no electricity, water or gas for civilian use. The CNN news network, holed up in the Al Rashed Hotel in Baghdad, gave extensive coverage (subject to Iraqi censorship) of the war. Its reporter Mr Peter Arnett became known world-wide.

If the allied air offensive was hampered by anything it was sandstorms and rains, rather than by Iraqi opposition. The Iraqi attacks, either by the Iraqi air force or by Scud missiles using chemical, nuclear or biological warheads, never came.

By the end of 1990 Saddam had released the last of the hostages but he switched his tactics to environmental terrorism by pumping over 4 million barrels of oil into the Gulf from Kuwait. A huge oil slick, 35 miles long and 15 miles wide, threatened the coast of Kuwait and areas further down the Gulf. The US forces used 'smart' bombs to bomb the oil pipelines and thus eventually controlled this oil flow, but catastrophic damage, some perhaps irreparable, was done to the fragile ecology of the Gulf.

Anti-aircraft guns had been positioned on buildings and flyovers in Kuwait since early January 1991. Pillboxes were erected at prominent places and a black-out of street lighting put in force. Saddam himself made two visits to Kuwait to bolster the sagging morale of his troops in January 1991.

As the air war intensified, so did the Iraqi terror tactics within Kuwait. The Kuwaiti nationals were pulled from the streets to be used as hostages; Iraqi sappers built fire lines or barricades of trenches, minefields and moats of oil. They also mined the oilfields and oil installations, refineries, power stations and desalination plants. A total of over 5 million mines were planted on land and in the sea.

The Kuwaitis and expatriates in Kuwait had long anticipated an eventual war of liberation. As early as September 1990 there was a rumour of the use of poison gas by Iraq. In early January 1991 'Kuwait Message', a television programme broadcast from other Gulf states, started giving 'do it yourself' lessons on how to face a war, such as building sandbag shelters, storing tinned food, and first aid, and even the use of Atropine serum as an antidote for poison gas.

While the air war raged on, waiting for the start of the

ground offensive, diplomatic activity intensified. Peace efforts were made by Iran through its President Rafsanjani but to no avail. Mr Gorbachev's envoy, Mr Primakoff, met Saddam Hussein. After his return to Moscow, a Soviet proposal for defusing the crisis was announced. It included the following:

1 Iraq to agree to a full and unconditional withdrawal from Kuwait.
2 This withdrawal to start the second day after cessation of hostilities.
3 Withdrawal to be completed within a fixed time frame.
4 After the withdrawal of two-thirds of the Iraqi forces from Kuwait, the United Nations economic sanctions to be lifted.
5 After complete withdrawal, the United Nations to pass a ceasefire Resolution.
6 After the ceasefire, all POWs to be released.
7 Withdrawal to be monitored by countries not involved in the conflict and so authorised by the United Nations.

The Soviet proposal did not touch upon the restoration of the Kuwait Government or the issue of war reparations.

The Iraqi regime's response was sent through Mr Tariq Aziz to Moscow on 21 February 1991, and contained new clauses. The Iraqi conditions for withdrawal were:

1 Ceasefire to be effective before pullout.
2 Coalition forces to leave the Gulf within one month.
3 Patriot missiles to be removed from Israel.
4 Compensation to Iraq for war damages.
5 An Israeli withdrawal from occupied Palestinian territory.
6 The Amir of Kuwait should not be restored.
7 Foreign countries to cancel Iraqi debt.
8 Iraq to have a say in post-war security arrangements.
9 No bases of outside forces in the Gulf.
10 The repeal of United Nations Resolutions and sanctions against Iraq.

Obviously, this was unacceptable to the allied coalition, especially the USA. Militarily, having a ceasefire before withdrawal was unacceptable. Moreover, the Iraqi response did not mention future security of Kuwait, and sanctions should remain until war reparations were paid by Iraq.

Iraq's proposals were also unacceptable to Israel, as these

would leave Saddam still in power and in full control of his weaponry. He would effectively emerge from the crisis as a hero.

THE GROUND WAR AND THE LIBERATION OF KUWAIT

By the middle of February, preparations for the ground war were complete as all peace efforts had failed. USA began to withdraw its diplomats from Iraq and activated its reservists. Over 1,300 tanks, 1,100 armoured vehicles and 1,100 artillery pieces in Iraq and Kuwait had been destroyed by the allied bombing. Meanwhile, Iraq announced that it would form an independent government in Kuwait (i.e. a tacit admission on the part of Iraq that Kuwait was not the 19th province of Iraq). It also commenced rounding up over 10,000 Kuwaitis to be taken to Iraq and stepped up its terrorist activities in Kuwait.

On 22 February 1991, President Bush gave an ultimatum to Iraq, until noon (5.00 p.m. Greenwich Mean Time) on Saturday 23 February 1991 to withdraw. He also talked to President Gorbachev moments before the deadline expired.

Iraq immediately responded by torching over 700 oil wells in Kuwait and by detonating the northern pier of Mina Al Ahmadi oil terminal, thereby adopting a 'scorched earth' policy.

The Iraqis knew that they were on the verge of defeat. Still the propaganda war increased in intensity through the 'Mother of Battles' radio station. Power was cut in Kuwait on 15 February, only to be restored within a day. It was cut off again on 24 February as Iraqi troops began sabotaging power stations. Water supplies were drastically reduced from 6 February 1991 and totally cut off four days later.

The ground war started in the early hours of Sunday 24 February 1991. Iraq was expecting an amphibious attack by over 20,000 marines on Kuwait but was surprised to face a ground attack from Saudi Arabia in the south. The US forces, with Saudi and Kuwaiti forces, advanced into Kuwait. On the left flank, US, French and British forces led the attack on the northern frontiers of Kuwait and southern part of Iraq, effectively cutting off any escape route for the Iraqi forces. These Iraqi forces were already a demoralised lot with communications to and supplies from Iraq cut off by the relentless bombing. Now their escape route was sealed.

The USS *Missouri*, along wih other ships, such as HMS *Gloucester*, lay off the Kuwaiti coast, pounding Iraqi positions as 2,000 paratroopers were airlifted 50 miles into Iraq by helicopters.

By the second day, 24 February 1991, a total of over 2,000 Iraqi tanks had been destroyed. Meanwhile, the US Seventh Marine Crops were in position in northern Iraq preventing the Republican Guards of the Iraqi army from moving south. The Republican Guards were the elite fighting force of Saddam Hussein. They were better paid, clothed, fed and trained than other divisions in the Iraqi army. There were more than 150,000 Republican Guards in Kuwait and southern Iraq among the 500,000 Iraqi troops, but they were outflanked and outmanoeuvred by the allied forces. The epic tank battles which had been expected never took place.

Around twenty-three divisions of the Iraqi army, comprising 260,000 Iraqi troops, were neutralised. By 26 February 1991 allied forces had recaptured Kuwait airport. Iraqi troops were surrendering in thousands and even the allied forces, which had prepared for mass Iraqi surrender, were unprepared for the scale on which it took place.

As soon as the ground war began, Iraqi troops in Kuwait were ordered to leave. The withdrawal started on the night of Monday 25 February 1991. In most cases, the officers and senior ranks abandoned their troops, who were left without leadership or food. Many were poorly trained conscripts and they resorted to wholesale looting and arson, as well as murder, in the city of Kuwait before they left in panic. The only road connecting Kuwait to Iraq passes over Al Mutlaa Ridge. Here they were sitting ducks for the allied air forces who picked them off at will. For about 10 kilometres this area was littered with dead soldiers and civilians, destroyed armour and looted equipment. This became a 'graveyard' for Iraqis and 'Saddamiyat Al Mitlaa', as it was called by the Iraqis, will remain a stigma on Saddam's face as long as he lives.

7

KUWAIT: THE AFTERMATH OF WAR AND THE REBUILDING CHALLENGE

THE FIRST 90 DAYS – THE EMERGENCY PROGRAMME

After seven months of occupation and war the elements of Kuwait's infrastructure were still intact, as the expected hand-to-hand battle never took place. But Iraqi vandalism and sabotage while fleeing the allied advance meant reconstruction could take as long as ten years. In the oilfields, Saddam's soldiers had ignited 732 oil wells and left the rest of the world to bear the economic and environmental cost.

Kuwait immediately embarked on a three-stage programme of restoration – Emergency, Recovery and finally Reconstruction. The emergency stage covered the reconnection of basic services and the clearing and temporary repair of Government and state buildings. This was completed within the 90-day stipulated period.

When allied troops evicted the Iraqi army, they entered a battered country virtually without food, drinking water, electricity and telephone service. Within two months these four features of everyday life were made available. During these months, small armies of engineers, electricians, plumbers and construction workers removed most of the physical reminders of Iraqi occupation, from painting over pro-Iraq slogans on ministry buildings to removing Soviet made T–52 tanks from schoolyards. They hauled away or demolished the carcasses of some 3,000 burned Iraqi tanks and vehicles, 400 pillboxes, 260 bunkers and 600 concrete barriers, all within three months.

More than 200 kilometres of highways and city streets were repaved. A Saudi construction firm repaved the Kuwait International Airport, heavily strafed by allied bombers, and removed 700 vehicles and the wreckage of a British Airways 747 that was blown up shortly after the invasion.

Retreating Iraqi troops had dynamited electricity generating facilities and sabotaged sub-stations, power lines and transformers on 23 February, and left Kuwait City without power or water. Working round the clock for three weeks, engineers and electricians of the US Corps of Engineers restored power on 23 March and repaired Kuwait's two main control stations, 4,800 kilometres of fallen or damaged power lines, 300 looted sub-stations, and hundreds of transformers ruined by Iraqi soldiers who had punctured them with rifle fire.

Within weeks, most of the desalination plants and main water lines were back in service, providing more than 100 million gallons of water per day, and a 2 billion gallon reservoir restored. Telephone services, virtually non-existent after liberation, were restored to over 90 per cent of customers and the country's international call capability expanded rapidly. Television stations and radios began broadcasting again and the first of the pre-war newspapers, *Al Qabas*, began publishing after quickly replacing sophisticated printing machinery the Iraqis had removed on 16 January, only hours before the allied air campaign started.

The US Corps of Engineers, after restoring essential services, moved to refurbishing damaged and gutted buildings, the Parliament building and royal palaces. Thousands of Kuwaitis started returning home, brought in by special flights.

Meanwhile, the Central Bank of Kuwait imposed a limit of KD 4,000 per account for cash withdrawals. This was increased to KD 6,000 in July 1991, and the limit was dispensed with altogether from August 1991.

All eight locally incorporated banks started operations within weeks of liberation, but with reduced staff and a limited branch network.

THE RECONSTRUCTION PHASE

This phase was planned to last over a year. Initially it was thought that reconstruction costs would total more than $100 billion. This figure was later whittled down to $20 billion. Electricity, water and the internal road system were all put in order at the cost of $130 million, a fraction of the amount originally estimated.

As the pre-invasion population of 2 million had been halved, effectively Kuwait now has a surplus of buildings in spite of the number damaged in the war.

The biggest contract awarded up to 1992 had been to the US-based Bechtel Corporation for providing support services in fire fighting. This amount to $500 million. In fact, the business bonanza was far less than anticipated as, in spite of the vandalism and looting, there was not the amount of physical destruction as was first thought (after all, Saddam intended to occupy Kuwait, not destroy it!).

There have been no big contracts awarded except in the oil sector and for the supply of basic consumer goods. The Government simply started to help the rebuilding of the local private sector by giving contracts to Kuwaitis where possible.

THE OIL INFERNO

This was a disaster unparalleled in history. Kuwait's 732 blazing or gushing oil wells posed the most daunting task after the liberation. Initially, the Government stood helplessly by as oil worth an estimated $120 million shot into the blackened skies each day. This constituted a daily loss of 4 to 6 million barrels of oil reserves. Initially, three Texas fire fighting organisations, including the legendary Red Adair, and a Canadian group were called in. Soon the number of teams was expanded to twenty-eight, with teams from Britain, France, Romania, China, Soviet Union, Iran and even Kuwait.

The standard procedure was to inundate a site with water to cool it, then to rake built up coke and other debris from around the wellhead. The fire was then extinguished using special smokestack-like tubes and more water and the well was then capped and sealed.

Initially, it was estimated that it would take more than two years, i.e. well into 1993, to put out all the wells. This forecast was reduced to about a year as more teams were drafted in, and in fact the last fire was extinguished on 6 November 1991. The last to be put out was Well Burgan 118, ceremoniously extinguished by HH the Amir amidst great scenes of rejoicing.

Before the final fires were extinguished, Kuwait had already recommenced oil shipments. The first shipment of crude since the Gulf war was loaded into the Norwegian tanker *Thorness* on 27 July 1991. This was 261,000 tons of crude, or almost 2 million barrels (it must be recalled that before the Iraqi invasion, Kuwait's oil production quota was 1.5 million barrels per day). By August 1991, Kuwait's oil production had reached 115,000 barrels per day from the Maqwa and Burgan fields. In addition, it was getting half of the flow from the so-called 'Neutral Zone' shared with Saudi Arabia. The zone's production was 200,000 barrels per day.

In mid-September 1991 Kuwait started drilling new oil wells in the Ahmadi Oilfield through Sante Fe International, a wholly owned subsidiary of the Kuwait Oil Company. By then, Kuwait's biggest refinery at Mina Al Ahmadi had resumed operations. This refinery has a capacity of 370,000 barrels per day and resumption enabled Kuwait to cease importation of all refined products, including gasolene and fuel for power and desalination plants. All units were expected to be on stream by mid-1992.

During the occupation, Iraqi soldiers had barricaded themselves in Mina Al Ahmadi and the refinery had been damaged during the war. By December 1991, the second refinery, Mina Al Abdulla, came back on stream at the rate of 100,000 barrels per day. This rose to 156,000 barrels per day in January 1992. The main control room of this refinery had been packed with explosives and blown up by Iraqi soldiers as the allies advanced at the end of February 1991. As at July 1992, Kuwait's third refinery at Shuaiba was unlikely to resume operations in the foreseeable future. Its only crude unit was put out of action and a decision had not been taken as to whether to repair it or to build a new one.

The revamping of the first two refineries was being undertaken in two stages. The first stage to bring Mina Al Ahmadi and Mina Al Abdulla up to their previous capacities, and the second to upgrade them to produce top-grade products such as low-sulphur fuel oil for export. Both stages were due for completion in 1992 or early 1993.

By September 1991, Kuwait had started to tackle the large pools and lakes of crude oil in areas where damaged wells had been gushing uncontrollably. The oil was retrieved, treated and either blended with crude produced from wells and then sold or else sold in its retrieved state. Around 10 to 15,000 barrels per day were being handled in this manner.

ENVIRONMENTAL CATASTROPHE

The environmental terrorism unleashed by Saddam Hussein's retreating troops – torching oil wells and blowing oil pipelines – has resulted in what some experts have called the world's biggest environmental catastrophe. The crude particles, noxious gases, and smoke from the fires led to widespread increase in asthma, eye allergies and infections of the human respiratory system. During the initial months after the invasion, the fires did not seem to pose a great threat but whenever the fumes blew over the city, cloaking it in semi-darkness, many residents complained of nausea, headaches and breathing problems.

Luckily, the city enjoyed reasonably clean air in summer 1991, because the wind blew the smoke eastward towards the Gulf or south, towards Saudi Arabia and Bahrain. But when the wind changed direction, the residents of Kuwait City choked on a swirling cocktail of sand and smoke. Pharmacies were unable to stock masks and inhalers in sufficient quantity to keep pace with the demand and hospitals received a steady stream of asthmatics fearing a respiratory collapse due to the appalling pollution. By the middle of summer 1991, initial reports indicated smoke clouds over the Gulf covering an area of 5,800 square miles and rising to a height of 150,000 feet. There were reports of smoke 1,600 miles south and south east of the wells with regional temperature distortions up to 625 miles away.

In Kuwait, when the smoke cloud was at its most dense, animals were found to be dying in the desert. The air temperature was 10 to 15 degrees Celsius below normal.

The effects were by no means confined to Kuwait, however. Iraq experienced black rain, lower regional temperatures and shortened crop-growing seasons. Extensive particle fallout and a rise in water acidity affecting crops and forests was reported.

In Saudi Arabia, there was much pollution from smoke and black rain. In Iran, black rain was being reported from March 1991 onward in Dezful in the north and Kernan, Shiraz Genarch and Busheir in the south. Smoke was also reported in the desert and there were fears of lower regional temperatures and a shortening of the growing season. Soot was being deposited in mountain ranges and washed into water supplies, and there was a long-term threat to 2.5 million hectares of semi-arid forests around the Gulf and the Sea of Oman.

Smoke and pollution was affecting the United Arab Emirates and neighbouring states in the lower Gulf, while Afghanistan reported pollution from black rain and smoke, and Pakistan reported that black rain had been frequently experienced in Baluchistan province. In India, skiers in the Himalayan mountains reported black snow, two inches thick, in Kashmir. These reports gave rise to fears of serious flooding due to a premature melting of the snow. Black rain and smoke were reported in the southern areas of the former USSR, in Bulgaria and Turkey, where early in March 1991 the Governor of Adana State ordered residents not to use rain water or to drink it as soot deposited in the mountains had washed into water supplies.

After Kuwait, the next greatest environmental catastrophe was experienced on the eastern Gulf coast of Saudi Arabia, from Khafji to Jubail. The war has destroyed Saudi Arabia's north-eastern coast. According to leading international environmental groups, 400 kilometres of the Saudi coast are beyond repair. Animals and birds have died in large numbers and tar balls have littered beaches plastered with oil. Large numbers of diseased fish with fin rot and skin ulcers have been reported and in some areas a sticky mix of oil, bacterial slime and rotting algae was left on the shore, well above the high water mark. Each time a bird dived for food, it would be coated in oil, and birds trying to find food on the beaches continually ingested oil.

An estimated 6 to 8 million barrels of oil were spilled during the Gulf War and was deposited on the shore or sank to the sea bottom. There, it provides an even greater long-term hazard. By covering the aquatic vegetation it robs the water of vital oxygenation. The vegetation rots, releasing toxic gas and poisons into the marine environment which destroy fish and animal life alike. Many species are unique to the Gulf, while others have evolved mutations peculiar to the Gulf's aquatic conditions. These are lost for ever.

Scientists studying the Saudi coast have found oil in sand up to 30 centimetres deep between the high and low water marks. Saudi Arabia's Meteorological and Environmental Protection Agency (MEPA) removed a major portion of the oil floating near the coast, and while much of Saudi Arabia's offshore coral and sea grass beds, a major spawning ground for fish and shrimp, may have escaped immediate damage, the build-up of toxic elements from suspended oil and putrefaction could well cause long-term havoc, as mentioned above.

THE ENVIRONMENT IN KUWAIT

Opinions on effects on Kuwait's environment have been sharply divided. Mr William Keilly, head of the US Environment Protection Agency, claimed that there was no acute health problem due to air pollution, but the long-term health implications were not yet known. The US National Science Foundation backed his views after conducting thirty-five research flights. According to them, natural cleaning processes would prevent a disastrous build-up of pollution from the burning oil wells, and in any case these have all been extinguished for some time.

But other environmentalists allege that the oil fire damage is being downplayed. According to Dr Ali Khuraibet, a founder member of the Kuwait Environment Action Team (KEAT), 'our environment has not been damaged, it has been ruined.' A similar opinion was given by Dr David Snashall of the Commonwealth Health Department.

He warned that the gasses and particles from the oil wells would affect health over the long-term. He predicted a jump in lung cancer among Kuwaitis within one or two decades. Sulphur dioxide, the prime constituent of acid rain, turned wrecked vehicles into rusting hulks, and when mixed with mucus it has a similar corrosive effect on lung tissue, permanently damaging the lungs.

In August 1991 a conference was organised in Harvard University by the Arab Fund for Social and Economic Development with the participation of the World Health Organisation (WHO) and the United Nations Programme for the Protection of the Environment (UNEP), and several other scientific establishments around the world. On the basis of data available, the conference recommended urgent measures be taken to prevent the effects of pollution on human life. According to the confer-

107

ence, short-term effects, visible within a year, would include an increase in the mortality rate by 10 per cent – especially among the elderly and children. Long-term effects were held to be more complicated and difficult to predict or define. However, they accepted as a well established scientific fact that exposure to such a high concentration of oil pollutants will cause respiratory and ophthalmic diseases, as well as a general loss of vigour.

Scientists at the conference expected at least 1,000 of the existing population in the area in general to have shorter age spans but others put the figure as high as 50,000. These high expectations were based on past experience and scientific data collected on humans, animals, water, etc., that were affected by the fallout and subsequent pollution stemming from the Chernobyl episode. Although the pollution itself was different in nature, the long-term effects of oil fires may well be more disastrous than Chernobyl, the scientists warned. Accordingly, they recommended that immediate steps be taken to contain and decrease the anticipated ill-effects. Other scientists have recommended taking further protective measures, such as information campaigns to spread awareness of the dangers of being exposed to such pollutants, and the establishment of early warning systems to warn the public when pollution levels are high and to ensure that they don appropriate protective gear.

The international environmental group Greenpeace also warned that the massive amounts of sulphur dioxide, carbon monoxide and oxides of nitrogen spewed into the atmosphere would have serious long-term effects, including pulmonary infection, lung and skin cancer, and eye damage. According to them, the levels of carcinogenic hydrocarbons over Kuwait City were at levels eighty times the acceptable limit set by the US Environment Protection Agency. Greenpeace's monitoring team also found severe damage to Kuwait's fragile desert ecology. It is estimated that between 50 and 75 per cent of Kuwait's land surface is covered in a thick oil soot, and the desert's thin protective crust, severely damaged by the movement of heavy military vehicles, has been badly impacted. Much of the vegetation which acted as an anchor for the sand had been killed by the fallout from the oil fires. According to Dr Fatima Abdalai, a scientist with the Kuwait Environmental Action Team

(KEAT) who briefed the Greenpeace team, 'everything is contaminated in Kuwait. Even though the oil fires are put out, the real environmental problems will stay with us at least for twenty to thirty years.'

The Greenpeace team worked in concert with the KEAT team mentioned earlier. This is basically a non-Government environmental group in Kuwait, formed by concerned scientists from the Kuwait Institute of Scientific Research (KISR). They undertake both marine and air pollution investigations.

THE HUMAN TRAGEDY

If the Iraqi invasion produced an environmental catastrophe, it also produced a human tragedy of torture, terror and trauma.

There have been countless tales of physical brutality and torture of men, women and children during the occupation period. These include killing and raping in front of relatives, electric shocks and mutilation of organs. Some have been documented but many, although known to close friends and family members, have not been, as the victims, especially women, do not come forward to relate their experiences, due to the fear of social stigma.

During 1991 Kuwait's Hospital of Psychological Medicine continued to receive 150 to 180 outpatient cases a day. This, according to Dr Buthayana A. Mughawi, a clinical psychologist attached to the hospital, is a 'definite increase' taking into account the present population of Kuwait. Moreover, the patients definitely needed not only medicine but psychological treatment as well. Psychologists also state that the trend towards fast driving, bouts of anger for trivial things, and general laxity in social behaviour are all manifestations of pent-up anger, which when suppressed can lead to violence. The results could be seen in the media reports of violence in street and schools after the liberation of Kuwait.

Doctors say that apart from victims of torture, imprisonment and rape, there are Kuwaitis who have trouble dealing with the way the invasion disrupted their peaceful lives and affected their economic health. They suffer from frustration and depression. Social worker Latifa Al Rageeb stated that the crime rate has increased by 48 per cent since liberation. Moreover, it is not just an increase in quantity, the nature of crimes has changed with an increase in murder, possession of weapons, arson and theft. Many Kuwaitis – some of whom fought in the resistance against Iraq – have hung on to weapons they confiscated from the fleeing Iraqi troops, and these are a constant threat to law and order.

Mental health specialists add that their task is complicated by the tradtional reserve towards mental health care among Kuwaiti nationals, although these reservations are receding. These unfortunate people suffer from depression, nightmares, anxiety, lack of concentration, nervousness, isolation from society and no interest in work or family life.

Dr Al Maghawi, cited earlier, recounted the story of a 32-year-old man. When he was released from an Iraqi jail in March 1991, he returned to Kuwait and tried unsuccessfully to kill himself. He later told doctors that he was repeatedly raped by Iraqi soldiers. A few weeks later he learnt that Iraqi soldiers had raped his wife while he was imprisoned. He could not stand the shame and tried to kill himself a second time.

Yet another manifestation of the human tragedy was revealed by a survey carried out by the United Nations Childrens Fund (UNICEF). The study showed that 62 per cent of Kuwaiti children have suffered psychological shock as the result of the invasion and war. They had seen the bodies of people they knew either hanging or lying on the streets. Fifty per cent of the children studied were having repeated nightmares and suffered a lasting feeling of fear.

Dr Hassan Al Ibraheem, Chairman of the Kuwait Society for the Advancement of Arab Childhood (KSAAC) and a former Minister of Education, cited the example of an 11-year-old girl who had seen the body of her neighbour's son thrown on the ground. After the liberation the girl began suffering from repeated nightmares, one to three times a week, in which she saw him standing above her and asking her why she did not cover him.

There were other children, who when asked 'what they would like to be?' stated that they would like to become soldiers. In drawing competitions when children were asked to draw what they liked, they did not draw a family or the Kuwait Towers or a scene – instead they drew tanks, dead bodies and planes.

Hence, the reconstruction of Kuwait should not only be

directed at the country's physical infrastructure, but at the individual citizen also. The United Nations has decided that Iraq should pay the victims of mental abuse and anguish. Those to be compensated include the hostages that Iraq held as human shields, those tortured or raped or forced into hiding, those who had a spouse, child or parent who died or suffered a personal injury, or those who were deprived of all economic resources so that their survival or that of their family was seriously threatened.

OUR PRISONERS OF WAR

Yet another aspect of the human tragedy which must not be forgotten is our missing prisoners of war. Over 800 Kuwaitis are, at the time of writing, missing, and it is not known whether they are dead or alive. But efforts are still actively being pursued to track them and, if alive, to free them.

POLITICAL POLARISATION

A wider consequence of the invasion and liberation has been the polarisation of the Arab world. While Iraq obviously became the 'Pariah' or the 'outcast' and was seen to be supported by Jordan, Yemen, Sudan and Palestine, the nations of the Gulf Consultative Council have started to forge stronger relationships with Iran, and Syria and Egypt are now considered staunch allies, having contributed to Operation Desert Storm. Even Israel is seen by some as being 'not so bad after all'.

Since the rout of Iraq, Kuwait's main concern has been to formulate a defence policy that would guarantee its safety. There is still a fear of Iraq, and Kuwait sees the United States and the West as its only guarantee of security. An agreement in March 1991 between Kuwait, its Gulf Arab allies, Egypt and Syria to set up a Pan Arab Force, collapsed after months of wrangling about the size, cost and role of the force. Under the proposed agreement, or the Damascus Declaration as it was called, Egypt and Syria would have provided the bulk of the force but it would be financed by Arab Gulf states. Kuwait also wanted a permanent US presence in Kuwait, but this was not forthcoming either. So a ten-year defence pact has been concluded with the USA, whereby Kuwait and US forces would conduct joint military manoeuvres, and the USA would store military equipment in Kuwait. Similar agreements have been made with the French and the British.

THE ROLE OF THE UNITED STATES

For the United States, the liberation of Kuwait undoubtedly resulted in manifold advantages:

1 It was a moral boost after the Vietnam débâcle.
2 It was able to secure a permanent military presence (though not a base) in the Middle East.
3 It was able to try its weapons in a real-life situation and measure their efficiency and effectiveness. The Patriot missile is a case in point.
4 It could bring Israelis and the Arabs 'closer' as Iraq became their 'common enemy'.
5 It could neutralise the Palestinian influence on the oil-rich countries of the Gulf. It could push Palestinians to the negotiating table, with Israel having the upper hand.
6 It could destroy Saddam Hussein's status as formidable Arab leader and destroy his huge army, which was a major threat to Israel.
7 It was assured, through its major contribution to the victory of the oil-rich Middle Eastern countries, gratitude that could be immensely valuable in future controversies over oil price rises.
8 It could create a major market for its arms. Many of the weapons brought into the area and not used in the War could be sold.
9 But certain questions still remain in the minds of many observers, especially those in the Arab world. The Americans defeated Iraq, but they did not go after Saddam Hussein. They could have taken him, had they wished, just as they had taken General Noriega of Panama and brought him to the USA. This they did not do perhaps because Iraq would have disintegrated without Saddam to hold it together, and Iran would then have risen as a fundamentalist super-power in the area without Iraq being strong enough to act as a counterbalance.

10 With the disintegration of the Soviet Union, and the economic downfall of the fragmented countries that evolved out of the Union, the USA was the only super-power left. This must be reasserted again and again and in this context it is pertinent to recall what Mr Alexander Haig, who was the former Secretary of State, said in Turkey a couple of years ago. 'The President of the USA asks the State Department to create confusion or problems somewhere in the world and then requests the Pentagon to solve it. This is the way we live.'

So, considering the host of advantages that accrued to the USA following the liberation of Kuwait, one cannot help but wonder if the USA had any prior knowledge of the Iraqi invasion, and if so why did it remain silent? Only a few days prior to the invasion, the Ambassador of the USA to Iraq, Mrs April Gillespie, had made supportive statements favouring the Iraqis. It is difficult to believe that the US Intelligence, with all the spy satellites and sophisticated equipment at its disposal, was unable to get a whiff of the ensuing invasion. The build-up of Iraqi forces on the border with Kuwait must have been monitored in detail, yet it was ostensibly discounted on more than one occasion as a bluff in Saddam's campaign to force Kuwait to support a rise in oil prices.

Although Saddam maintained his hold on Iraq, his grip tended to loosen after the war as he shifted cabinet and party members like pieces on a chessboard. Many more were dismissed or even executed.

Iraq was later allowed by the United Nations to sell up to $1.5 billion worth of oil, over a period of six months. Part of the proceeds were permitted to be used to buy foodstuffs, medicines, materials and supplies for certain essential needs, the remainder was to form part of a compensation fund to meet the cost of United Nations forces, the return of all Kuwaiti property and a half share of the costs of the Boundary Commission.

The United Nations also clamped rigid controls on Iraq to prevent it from ever again acquiring weapons of mass destruction after its existing arsenals were destroyed. It has imposed a highly intensive system of United Nations inspection to ensure that Baghdad does not rebuild the nuclear, biological, chemical or ballistic missile stocks and facilities already uncovered and scrapped by the United Nations.

Iraq has opposed previous security council decisions, sometimes to the point of sparking a crisis, such as when a United Nations nuclear inspection team was held in a Baghdad car park for four days in September 1991. But in each case, it has eventually backed down.

The United Nations monitoring scheme is of infinite duration and gives its inspectors the authority to move at will anywhere in Iraq by land or air, to remove or to photograph any items or documents, to take any samples, interview any personnel or install any necessary surveillance equipment. The teams also have the right to stop and inspect vehicles, ships and planes and to monitor Iraqi imports and exports.

Iraq is bound to co-operate fully, allowing the United Nations teams unimpeded access, complying with all their requests, and is required to enact legislation to prevent its own nationals from carrying out any activities banned under the United Nations Resolution. Periodic reports on nuclear, chemical, biological and missile related materials, facilities and activities must also be provided. Iraq is also barred from possessing a number of chemicals that the United Nations lists as having little or no use except as chemical warfare agents. Another list of chemicals with dual military and civil use is subject to specific regulations, as are radiocactive isotopes used for medical, agricultural or industrial purposes.

THE QUESTION: WHY?

Now that the war is behind us, and the reconstruction of Kuwait is well under way, we may pause to ask the question, why did Iraq embark on this adventure at all? As stated in Chapter 5, there could be one, or many reasons. But, as events demonstrated, Saddam miscalculated. The world did not stand aside as in the case of China's occupation of Tibet, or Israel's occupation of Palestinian land. It was Saddam's miscalculation that led to Iraq's downfall. However, there are other players in the drama who also stand to lose. These are the Palestinians, whom nobody wants to shelter now. All their contributions to Kuwait during the last twenty years have been negated by the shortsightedness of their leaders in siding with Iraq. They now

114

have nowhere to go except to Jordan. Even in Lebanon they have become unwelcome. The 230,000 Palestinians who fled during the occupation are not allowed to return to Kuwait and most of the 170,000 who remained have been fired from their jobs and have returned to Jordan. Jordan too has suffered as a result of what the west saw as their 'pro-Iraq' stance. On one hand the Jordanians now have to house the thousands of Palestinians who have Jordanian travel papers, and on the other the aid to Jordan from the west has been reduced to a trickle. There are also other losers, such as Yemen and Sudan, who both sided with Iraq. Yemenis and Sudanese are now no longer welcome in Kuwait.

In fact, the Gulf crisis has forced Kuwait to reassess the whole of its demographic policy with a view to achieving a more desirable population balance between Kuwaitis and non-Kuwaitis, and national planning is being totally recast with this in mind.

8

THE KUWAITI ECONOMY AFTER LIBERATION

AFTER LIBERATION

The banking sector

Most of Kuwait's banks were in trouble before the war erupted. Five of Kuwait's six banks had technically been insolvent since the Al Manakh collapse and were being nursed through the special Difficult Debt Settlement Programme, as explained earlier. The banks' exposure to Al Manakh was around KD 1.5 billion and they were bearing a further KD 4 to 5 billion in outstanding loans just prior to the invasion. The head of Al Shall Economic Bureau, Dr Jassem Al Saadoun, has calculated that they will be lucky to recover more than KD 1.5 billion.

Political considerations also weigh heavily on the banking sector, as the Government, after the liberation, decided to write off the personal debts of all Kuwaitis. These amounted to KD 1.5 billion. While the banks do not have to foot the bill, they still have to forego the interest they would have earned. At the same time, they are still expected to pay the interest on deposits for the period of Iraqi occupation.

Saadoun and others believe these factors will likely result in a 50 per cent drop in banking sector share prices, when Kuwait's Stock Market opens. Since the banking sector accounts for 80 per cent of the shares traded in 1989, the impact is sure to be felt throughout the whole of Kuwait's economy. Economists contend that the banks can only return to normality in tandem with the rest of the economy, especially the oil sector. But even after the oil sector is fully operational, other sectors crucial to the wellbeing of the banks, such as construc-

117

tion and trade, are still likely to remain depressed. The situation will not stabilise until normal life returns to the country, i.e. political stability, freedom of movement of capital and a revival in the productive sectors of the economy.

In the meanwhile, Central Bank control on the commercial banks has been increasing. Although capital flights have not been as bad as initially feared, commercial customers have been either unable or unwilling to pay outstanding debts while they await Government grants to cover the damage inflicted during the Iraqi occupation. According to Capital Intelligence, a Cyprus-based bank research unit, the shortfall in provision for doubtful debts is KD 2.2 billion – about double the KD 1.2 billion deficit before the war. Capital Intelligence reckons that even a doubling of the value of collateral for the loans would only reduce the under-provisioning by 40 per cent.

There are also many other doubtful assets in the banks' books. They have some KD 150 million of Third World loans and there is an exposure, estimated at KD billions, to Iraq. Although much of this may be official funds channelled on a Government to Government basis, some is assuredly with the commercial banking system. As a result, the Central Bank has examined a number of schemes to deal with bad debts. One is to set up an agency similar to the Resolution Trust Corporation in the USA which is being used to help finance the restructuring of the American Savings and Loan industry. The Kuwaiti agency would be guaranteed by the State, with all bank bad debts transferred to it and it would then issue bonds.

Another plan was for the Government to take over the banks' bad debts and issue them with bonds backed by reparation payments from Iraqi oil exports. This plan met with stiff resistance at various forums, like the 'Democratic Forum', which stated that the cost of the programme would be much higher than envisaged. It would amount to over KD 11 billion after twenty years and not more than KD 900 million would be collected. The main accusation was that the principal debts of 240 persons amounted to KD 3,770 million while the debt of 4,932 others totalled only KD 120 million. They rejected the claim that the big debtors included some of the major economic activists in the country who thus should be bailed out to put the national economy back on track. The forum stated that 'Kuwait's economy is based on oil, while the contributions of these large debtors to the national economy is minimal.' The forum also rejected the treating of debts caused by the Al Manakh crash and those resulting from the Iraqi invasion on an equal footing.

After long and heated discussion, covering three full sessions, the National Council eventually passed the Government's plan to buy the KD 6 billion (US$ 20 billion) bad debt by 41 votes to 14 with 2 absentions. Only 57 of the 75 members of the Council were present. The basic controversy was not whether or not to support the banks. The issue was whether or not the government will ever get back the money from the debtors.

Issuing the bond would take the Government to its KD 10 billion (US$ 34 billion) public borrowing ceiling when added to KD 3 billion (US$ 11 billion) worth of outstanding bills and bonds. The bond issue eventually received Cabinet approval on 9 May 1992, and the assent of HH the Amir within days thereafter.

Although this solves the bad debt problems of the banks, there are still other problems in the banking sector. All the banks have reduced their domestic branch networks as Kuwait's population is certain to be much smaller. In the future this will have a big impact on funding costs. They may have problems too with the restoration of their credit lines with international banks. When they attempt this they may be forced to pay more than hitherto. There are also staffing problems. Over a third of bank staff in Kuwait were Palestinians before the conflict. With the pressure on Palestinians to leave the country and the ban on any Palestinians returning to Kuwait, their business skills will be sorely missed. The banks have been trying to lure other GCC citizens to fill the vacuum, but so far have met with only limited success.

While the combined balance sheet of the banks is expected to be between 25 per cent to 40 per cent lower than that of 1989, because of the guarantee by the Kuwaiti Government, there is no danger of the banks collapsing. But with the 'albatross' of bad debts still around their necks, they will have a difficult task to become fully operational and show decent profits for some time yet.

The real estate sector

The real estate market plummetted after liberation, primarily due to the reduction in population from about 2 million before the war to less than 1 million. Around 200,000 apartments are estimated to be vacant.

Furthermore, the Government's policy of reducing the proportion of non-Kuwaitis from over 70 per cent to well below 50 per cent implies that the total population is likely to remain low. Various suggestions have been put forward to mitigate this, such as the Government utilising vacant buildings instead of constructing new ones, a ban on the issuing of new construction permits and the demolition of surplus buildings in certain areas. But no matter how much the Government accepts these suggestions, it will be the policy on expatriate population that will decide the fate of the real estate sector.

Educational sector

Kuwait's public schools were used as barracks for thousands of Iraqi soldiers during the occupation period. Most were looted and many of the graffiti-covered rooms were piled with trash, including unexploded grenades and mortar shells. More than 120 schools were too badly damaged in the war to be reopened in time to get the schools started. The US Army Corps of Engineers supervised major repairs to 150 schools. Britain brought in chemistry and physics laboratory equipment and UNESCO helped to develop special psychological counselling programmes. Egyptian publishing houses shipped in more than 10 million Arabic language text books and fleets of trucks from the Ministry of Education distributed them. Pupils will have two years of class compressed into one year, to make up for the school year loss. Post-war enrolment was around 250,000, compared with 400,000 before the war. This reduction is mainly due to the absence of Palestinian and Jordanian children.

Private schooling is available but the Government subsidy on it has been removed. Before the invasion, 100,000 pupils were enrolled in private schools, now there are only 13,000. Foreign schools have only 7,000 students, compared with 40,000 before the invasion.

The Government budget and the cost of reconstruction

The cost of reconstruction was originally expected to exceed US$ 100 billion immediately after liberation, but this was later scaled down drastically. By contrast, the cost of extinguishing the fires went up as top priority was given to this task. Originally it was believed that it would cost between half a million to one million dollars to extinguish each fire, but according to Al Shall Financial Consultancy Office's report, the actual cost was between a low of US$ 2.9 million to a high of US$ 410 million. Moreover, this report states that Kuwait could soon join the ranks of debtor countries. The state deficit, calculated as the difference between Kuwait's project spending and revenue over the next three years, was estimated at US$ 75 billion. The report states that the Government indicated that it would spend around US$ 85 billion over the period. US$ 22 billion would go to finance Operation Desert Storm, US$ 20 billion for the state budget (which is expected to be cut by 20 per cent) and another US$ 20 billion for the reconstruction of Kuwait, including defence expenditure, the cost of fighting oil well fires and the costs associated with the security pact arrangement.

It added that US$ 7 billion would need to go to bank loan write-offs to Kuwaiti citizens, another US$ 7 billion to cover Government borrowing from the private sector and US$ 7 billion to guarantee private deposits of local commercial banks. The Government also spent US$ 2 billion on Kuwaiti families during the occupation. All these total US$ 85 billion, while Kuwait's oil revenue is not likely to exceed US$ 10.5 billion in the next three years. The gigantic deficit of US$ 75 billion, according to the reports, may absorb Kuwait's financial reserves and foreign investments. This would put Kuwait among the debtor countries, a situation completely inconceivable but a few short years ago.

Thus, the report demands speedy action by the Government to ensure the country's economic future. It advocates that this should be done through reducing expenses and other financial commitments, or at least spreading them over a longer period of time.

As far back as July 1991, Kuwait had indicated that it wished to borrow US$ 33 billion to rebuild its war-shattered economy. A decree was issued by HH the Amir, instructing the Finance

Ministry to obtain the loans in various international financial markets. It was the first time that Kuwait – the Middle East's fourth largest oil exporter before the war – had asked international institutions for cash but, holding 10 per cent of the free world's proven oil resources, it was not expected to find much difficulty in raising money. It was the amount which surprised many economic analysts, who had predicted that Kuwait would seek loans of about US$ 10 billion.

Despite the Iraqi pillage, Kuwait has more than US$ 100 billion of overseas assets and Kuwait's decision to borrow abroad was to avoid upsetting international markets by a large selling-off of overseas assets. Any major selling would have left Kuwait without a financial cushion. According to Mr Abdulla Al Gabandi, Managing Director of the Kuwait Investment Authority, 'The muscle of Kuwait is our financial strength. If we sell our assets, we lose our strength.'

The Central Bank had since early July 1991 been issuing treasury bills and bonds. The Amiri decree had stated, 'The borrowing will be effected . . . without restricting it to the issue of treasury bills and bonds in the local market, but by borrowing in various international financial markets also.'

The US$ 33 billion will not be borrowed at once but will be spread over a period of time. The first big tranche was for US$ 5 billion, to be repayable over five years, through J. P. Morgan and Company. This was the largest single loan of its type ever to be raised by a sovereign borrower. Raising this money was not a problem but the pricing negotiations took time as Kuwait wanted the same rate as that applied to Saudi Arabia, i.e. 0.5 per cent over LIBOR (London Interbank Offer Rate).

International bankers argued that Kuwait will be unable to borrow as cheaply as Saudi Arabia. Under the Basle international capital adequacy rules, which stipulate that banks must set aside various amounts of capital when they make loans according to the status of the borrower, Kuwait had a full risk weighting while Saudi Arabia was zero rated. Hence the rate for Kuwait was to be between ¾ and 1 per cent greater.

The questions uppermost in the banks' minds while discussing long-term loans to Kuwait are:

1 Would Kuwait be prepared to use some of its existing assets

as security? If so, it will be able to borrow more cheaply, but the indication so far is that Kuwait would not.

2 Who would lend to Kuwait? As already indicated, Kuwait has a full risk weighting. This may deter banks like the Japanese banks, which have had their capital base undermined by the recent (1991) Tokyo market slide. However, Japanese bankers are reported as not regarding this as a serious obstacle as the pricing should take this into account.

3 What form will Kuwait's borrowing take? Kuwait may opt for a combination of export related credits and some general syndicated credits. Export-related credit arrangements have already been entered into with the Exim bank of USA. Kuwait may also opt for a series of one-year facilities which would eliminate some of the political risk. These could supplement three- and five-year syndicated loans.

In fact, Kuwait has already negotiated such short-term financing. A US$ 500 million facility has been negotiated with Citibank, while the Abu Dhabi based Arab Monetary Fund has granted a US$ 3.3 million loan to finance track operations.

The Islamic banks of the region are reported to be setting up a US$ 500 million loan fund. In this, the Islamic Development Bank in Jeddah is expected to put up US$ 60 million, Al Baraka Investment and Development Company of Saudi Arabia another US$ 80 million, Qatar Islamic Bank US$ 5 million, the Malaysian Chamber of Commerce US$ 8 million, and a further US$ 5.5 billion loan from the World Market is also under consideration.

9

THE FUTURE

KUWAIT: THE FUTURE OF THE ECONOMY

The future course of the Kuwaiti economy, as reconstruction takes place, will be based on both economic and political factors.

Economic factors

The prime factor here is oil: how much can Kuwait produce, how much can it sell as its OPEC quota and at what price? Kuwait entered the second quarter of 1992 with an output of 650,000 barrels per day, and was on target to reach its pre-invasion OPEC quota of 1.5 million barrels per day by the end of 1992. According to Mr Nasser Al Rawdhan, the Finance Minister, oil revenues for the whole of 1992 are expected to reach KD 2 billion, and for 1993 KD 3 billion. But these figures are based on the current level of oil prices and the assumption that the OPEC quota fixed for Kuwait will remain unchanged.

By contrast, the total spent on Operation Desert Storm, the capping of the oil wells and resettling of Kuwaitis, etc., is already US$ 35 billion. This obligation has been met by using bonds, deposits and equities totalling US$ 25 billion, while another US$ 5 billion has come from income from foreign investments, the remainder from international borrowings. As the oil revenues are only expected to be around KD 3 billion (or US$ 10 billion) by 1993, it would seem next to impossible for Kuwait not to have to liquidate the best part of its foreign investments, estimated to be about US$ 100 billion, if it keeps spending at the same rate. It may be forced to sell its 14 per cent stake in Daimler Benz, 5 per cent stake in British Petroleum, etc. As already indicated, internally the Government plans to clear KD 7 billion or US$ 25 billion of bad debts from local commercial banks in return for an extraordinary sale of Government bonds, repayable in twenty years. Although this would clear the banking system problems at a stroke, some economists fear that the US$ 20 billion price tag, the largest single clearance of bank debts in history, would seriously test the Government's cash flow. The overall fear is that the US$ 100 billion foreign assets would be depleted to below US$ 40 billion as a result of all these measures.

Many economists are now arguing that the country is spending an inordinate amount on bad debts, weapons and costly contracts without first establishing a set of priorities, and is giving excessive grants to people, putting an added strain on the country's exchequer.

The political factors

The prime mover of any economy is the demand for goods and services. Prior to the invasion Kuwait was home to a million and a half expatriates. Now it is planned to limit the population to half a million Kuwaitis and half a million expatriates. This would mean that the number of expatriates would be a third of the pre-invasion total. Also, the pre-invasion expatriates were mainly Palestinians, who spent a major part of their income and saved little. In future it will be mainly Egyptians and south-east Asians, who spend little and save or remit more. Thus this change in the number and the composition of the population is expected to bring a substantial fall in demand for accommodation, goods and services.

Although, as the clean-up of the banking system is effected, Kuwaitis will have their loans stretched over the longer term, they will have a reduced cash income due to the reduction in real estate income (fewer expatriates mean fewer apartments and shopping complexes being rented) and lower share prices (as explained earlier, bank shares form a major proportion of shares traded in Kuwait and their prices are expected to come down due to the clean-up and the reduced demand for bank services).

All this implies that the Kuwaitis themselves will have to

become more frugal and self-reliant. They will have to depend less on cheap expatriate labour and perform more of the tasks they had hitherto delegated to hired servants. This in turn implies that Kuwaiti women will inevitably start to play a more active and equal role in the economy, a right which they have been long demanding, together with the right to vote.

Finally, the Government will have to be less paternalistic and protective towards its citizens, who need to be exposed to a competitive environment if they are to face future developments with confidence. The proposal to privatise various sectors, starting with the country's telecommunications, is a step in the right direction but only a small first step. Kuwait is what Japan and Germany were around fifty years ago, with war-ravaged economies. We hope and pray that Kuwait too will rise like a phoenix from the ashes, as did these two leading nations of the world.

INDEX